CRIME AND MADNESS

ALSO BY THOMAS MAEDER

Antonin Artaud (in French)
The Unspeakable Crimes of Dr. Petiot

CRIME
AND MADNESS

THE ORIGINS AND EVOLUTION
OF THE INSANITY DEFENSE

THOMAS MAEDER

1817

HARPER & ROW, PUBLISHERS, New York

CAMBRIDGE, PHILADELPHIA, SAN FRANCISCO, LONDON
MEXICO CITY, SÃO PAULO, SINGAPORE, SYDNEY

FIRST EDITION

Designer: Barbara DuPree Knowles

Library of Congress Cataloging in Publication Data

Maeder, Thomas.
    Crime and madness.

    Bibliography: p.
    Includes index.
    1. Insanity—Jurisprudence—United States.
2. Criminal liability—United States. I. Title.
KF9242.M28   1985   345.73′04   84–48610
ISBN 0–06–015435–7   347.3054

    85 86 87 88 89 RRD 10 9 8 7 6 5 4 3 2 1

To LeRoy and Albertine
and, as always,
to Shawn

CONTENTS

Acknowledgments

I am indebted to David Bazelon, Robert Sadoff, and Ralph Slovenko, who helped me wend my way through some of the issues discussed in this book and who very generously read and commented upon the manuscript. They are responsible for valuable improvements: I alone am to blame for any errors. Innumerable others contributed in various ways to the writing of this book, but I would particularly like to thank those few whose friendship or hospitality, even more than their considerable practical help, made a sometimes arduous project enjoyable: Perry Berman, Barry Floyd, Natalie Greenberg, Michael Keedy, Ames Robey, Gare Smith, and Juanita Kidd Stout.

them to return to the society they victimized."[1] The Secretary of the Treasury called the situation "beyond belief" and "absolutely atrocious," while President Reagan himself remained diplomatically silent except to remark, while plugging a federal "anti-crime" bill, that the insanity defense had been "much misinterpreted and abused" and required "common-sense revisions."[2] A host of U.S. senators joined in the clamor for reform, and within weeks of the Hinckley verdict a Senate Judiciary Subcommittee held six hearings to discuss nine new bills proposing adoption of a "guilty but insane" or "guilty but mentally ill" verdict, or recommending the outright abolition of the insanity plea.

By early September, Judge Barrington D. Parker, who presided at Hinckley's trial, had received some 1,500 letters, nearly all of them protesting the verdict and castigating Parker personally and the system in general for permitting a legal grotesquerie that, according to one Alabama couple, made the American judicial system a laughingstock to the rest of the world.[3] Public fury was scarcely assuaged when John Hinckley himself, by then a forensic ward patient at St. Elizabeths Hospital, published an article in *Newsweek* calling the critics of his verdict "jealous" and "vindictive," and complacently instructing his readers that "sending a John Hinckley to a mental hospital instead of prison is the American Way."[4]

The circumstances of the Hinckley case might well have angered any thinking citizen, yet the verdict could easily have been shrugged off as a tolerable fluke except for a long-standing public misconception that the insanity defense is a problem of frequent occurrence, the judicial system having become a veritable sieve through which patently guilty and uniquely repulsive criminals, with no other conceivable defense, slip out on all sides, abetted by a conspiracy of defense lawyers and psychiatrists. Newspaper discussions of the insanity defense, both before and after the Hinckley affair, illustrated their arguments with especially colorful cases culled from the files:

former would-be or actual presidential assassins, weird torture-killers, the occasional crazed murderer who was released from a mental hospital only to kill again, and the exceedingly rare horror-movie variety of homicidal maniac who runs amok through the countryside with a hatchet. The circumstances of these dramatic crimes stick in one's mind long after a thousand equally horrible though, unfortunately, much more common-place murders, rapes, and beatings committed by supposedly sane and responsible citizens have faded from memory.

Public perception is at wide variance with reality. One astonishing 1979 study showing the extent to which this is true[5] asked Wyoming state legislators to guess what proportion of 21,012 felony indictments had resulted in an insanity acquittal. The average response was that insanity was raised in 4,458 cases and succeeded in 1,794. Laymen made guesses almost twice as high, estimating that 37 percent of felony defendants raised the insanity defense and more than 16 percent succeeded.[6] In fact, of those defendants, only 102—less than half of one percent—pleaded insanity, and a single person was acquitted for that reason.

Accurate statistics on insanity acquittals are almost impossible to find because courts frequently do not keep records on them, but available figures from other jurisdictions confirm that such acquittals are few, probably occurring in no more than one-fifth of one percent of terminated felony prosecutions.[7] Despite the post-Hinckley concern over federal insanity procedures, it turns out that in 1981 there were only four federal insanity acquittals.[8] Nationwide in 1978, the only year for which an accurate estimate has been made, approximately 1,625 defendants found not guilty by reason of insanity (NGRI) were committed to mental hospitals.[9] This number is small indeed in the context of more than a million violent crimes known to the police that year, including nearly twenty thousand murders and non-negligent homicides. Moreover, the average NGRI spends more time locked in a hospital after his acquittal than he would have spent in prison following a conviction.

Ordinarily NGRIs do not even fit the popular image of the criminally insane. Only a minority are acquitted of murder: percentages vary from state to state due to factors difficult to determine, but in New York 44 percent of NGRIs had been charged with homicide, in Michigan about 30 percent, in New Jersey near 20 percent, and in Oregon, which has one of the highest insanity acquittal rates in the country, contributing 103 of the nation's NGRIs in 1978, only 7 percent were acquitted of homicides. Moreover, these were neither crazed maniacs nor cunning fiends whom only a deluded and overpaid psychiatrist could call ill. David Berkowitz, Arthur Bremer, Squeaky Fromm, John Wayne Gacy, Charles Manson, Sara Jane Moore, Richard Speck, and Sirhan Sirhan all either dropped their insanity pleas or were convicted in spite of them.

The typical NGRI killer, if one can speak of such a thing, is the abused wife driven to distraction by years of physical and emotional torment who finally kills her husband, or the severely depressed person who kills his or her parents, children, lover, or spouse. They are people pushed to a unique and dreadful mental state, whom both common sense and medical science regard as more deserving of compassion and help than of punishment. Judges and juries, ordinarily so mistrustful of the insanity defense, view these defendants as outside the realm of blame but within the reach of sympathy. Even the prosecutor often does not oppose the insanity defense in such cases, and the only meaningful courtroom debate is over the appropriate dispositional conditions.

If the insanity defense is not the greatest practical problem facing our troubled criminal justice system, it nonetheless lies near the heart of moral and legal questions concerning society's rights and obligations toward those who violate the law. We punish willful transgressors, but for centuries we have held that it would be cruel to inflict punitive sanctions on someone who did not know that he was doing wrong. This leaves us with the awkward thesis that there is some theoretically definable point in the spectrum of human behavior, to one side of which criminal offenders are bad people who chose to do wrong, and to the other side of which they are unfortunate sufferers, compelled by forces beyond their control, whom society ought to nurse back to health. But where do we draw the line? Why should we excuse those who suffer from severe "mental illness," whatever that may be, but not those whose acts are driven by uncontrolled rage, excessive jealousy, wounded pride, overwhelming greed, a brutalizing childhood environment, or the other personality flaws that explain crimes of more normal criminals? Is the sorting out of the mentally culpable and the mentally innocent a legal or a medical problem, and to what extent does it and ought it to change in response to new scientific theories of human behavior?

Certain of the most serious difficulties with the insanity defense have arisen only recently. Until twenty years ago an insanity acquittal was a relatively facile show of compassion because, having found the defendant not criminally responsible, society was nonetheless confident that he would be locked in a mental institution for the rest of his life. But court decisions, psychoactive medications, and the availability of outpatient facilities then began a trend of emptying the large psychiatric hospitals of both civil and criminal patients, and for the first time large numbers of NGRIs could return to the streets as soon as their right to liberty outweighed their apparent need for hospital treatment. We were abruptly faced with a moral dilemma over just what we meant when we found insane criminals not responsible.

We do not wish to punish the truly mentally innocent—it would be Kafkaesque to imprison a man for a crime he knew nothing about or had been unable to prevent. On the other hand, the fact that a defendant was insane neither diminishes

1

THE ORIGINS OF THE
INSANITY DEFENSE

The ideal in a free society is that all of its members shall be equal under the law they have contrived to govern them, that they shall share the same rights and bear the same responsibilities, and that if they violate their laws they will be punished no differently than their fellows, and judged according to a collective sense of justice rather than by the passion and whim of individuals.

One could construct a very simple criminal code that would strictly prescribe one penalty for each offense, regardless of how or why the act had occurred. If a man were convicted of homicide it would not matter whether he had killed in the heat of passion, after cool deliberation, accidentally, in self-defense, or while dazed from a blow, intoxicated, or insane. Surely this system would treat people equally, but the most rudimentary human sympathies discern something askew in this recklessly equitable assignment of blame, and societies since the beginning of time have recognized that the fact of having committed an outlawed act was not, alone, necessarily synonymous with moral and legal culpability. As Justice Holmes said, "Even a dog distinguishes between being stumbled over and being kicked."[1]

It is comparatively easy to take into account such externally

1

verifiable extenuating or excusing circumstances as accident or self-defense. Circumstances vary greatly from one case to the next, but one can achieve a degree of consistency by judging them all according to what some hypothetical, normal, reasonable, and law-abiding citizen would have done under similar conditions. If this policy sacrifices some superficial rigor in the law, it strengthens the law's deeper purpose by expecting men to internalize their society's sense of values, and holding them responsible only for those things that they could have done or refrained from doing through the free and conscious exercise of those values.

It is far more difficult, however, to deal justly with variability, not in the act, but in the actor; to dole out, as one prominent judge has put it, "equal justice for the unequal." Members of society are not all equivalent, normal, reasonable beings who fit one hypothetical mold. Men differ in education, wealth, background, and values, and even in such fundamental factors as the strength of their emotions, their sense of compassion, their susceptibility to reason, and their capacity to feel duty or guilt.

If the law is to operate at all, and to maintain any pretense of egalitarianism, it must disregard these differences, but some are too great to ignore. The man who kills while defending himself against an imagined attack, or upon what he believes to be the transcendent command of God, or the idiot who cuts off his sleeping friend's head and then waits, giggling, to see his friend hunt for it when he wakes, none of these can be judged according to any hypothetical normal man who knew and chose to ignore the dictates of the law. One cannot ask how another man would have acted under similar circumstances, since such phantasmagoric circumstances could never exist for anyone else. To preserve the apparent equality of the rest, the law must segregate out these glaring aberrances— the flagrantly insane—whom a law based on moral responsibility and reason cannot touch. In the interests of protecting society as a whole, however, one wishes to keep this exceptional category as small as possible.

Throughout most of history there have been no specific criteria for exculpatory insanity; none, after all, were necessary in a relatively small community where everyone knew the offender. Ancient Hebraic law stated simply that idiots, lunatics, and children below a certain age ought not to be held criminally responsible, because they could not distinguish good from evil, right from wrong, and were thus blameless in the eyes of God and man. The fragmentary surviving Greek and Roman legal texts say nothing at all on the matter, though a section of Plato's *Laws* specifically provides that if a criminal defendant is senile, a child, or is proven insane, he should be responsible for no more than the payment of civil damages, "except that if he has killed someone and his hands are polluted by murder, he must depart to a place in another country and live there in exile for a year,"[2] and Marcus Aurelius is credited with the maxim that "madness is its own sole punishment."

In early Anglo-Saxon society there was strict liability for criminal acts, though virtually every crime was commutable by monetary compensation to the victim or his family, and a fine paid to the monarch for breach of the king's peace. Neither the fact that an offense took place by accident nor the insanity of the culprit affected the price tag of crime except that, in both cases, the families of homicide victims were denied the additional personal vengeance they were permitted to wreak upon willful murderers.

Under the influence of Augustinian theology, however, a blend of Christian ethics and Roman jurisprudence was infused into the laws of Britain, and a requirement for guilty intent gradually replaced strict liability and became a cornerstone of criminal law. The thirteenth-century legal scholar Henry de Bracton, who wrote the first comprehensive study of English law, indicated that it was for this reason that children and madmen cannot be guilty of crime. Both are innocent in their

3

designs and have no will to do harm, and a madman, he said, "knows not what he does and lacks mind and reason, and is not much removed from a brute."[3]

Accounts of early insanity cases are scarce and usually perfunctory, and it is difficult to make general statements based upon those that do exist. Bracton refers to a case around 1226 where a man named Ralph, who was "out of his wits and senses . . . killed a man and came before the justices and confessed that he had killed him . . . and he is in the prison, and will be for ever so long as he shall live, by order of the justices for that death."[4] Since at that time execution was the routine punishment even for much slighter offenses, and prisons were used only to detain the convicted pending final disposition, one must surmise that this life sentence was considered as lenient treatment.

Nigel Walker, who has intensively studied early English insanity laws, has discovered the lengthy account[5] of Richard Blofot of Cheddestan, who in 1270 went into a "frenzied seizure," attempted suicide, then murdered his wife and two children. The sheriff of Norfolk imprisoned Richard for six years on his own authority, but finally the case came to the attention of King Edward I, who asked that a jury be appointed to ascertain the facts of the case. "Richard is well enough," the jury advised, "but it cannot safely be said that he is so restored to soundness of mind that there would not be danger in setting him free, especially when the heat of summer is increasing, lest worse befall."

Eight years later, Hugh de Misyn was imprisoned at Nottingham for killing his daughter, but after inquiries were made, King Edward determined that "Hugh hanged his daughter whilst suffering from madness, and not by felony or of malice aforethought," and ordered him released to the custody of twelve men who would pledge to keep him under control.[6]

One knows, then, that there were acquittals, but one cannot accurately say under what conditions. There are no records to describe cases where lunacy was considered and dismissed. On the other hand, Richard of Cheddestan spent six years in jail before his case came to King Edward's attention, and there were undoubtedly many others, particularly those involving relatively minor crimes, that never reached trial at all, but were handled informally according to the discretion of the townsfolk and local authorities. Even when there was a formal trial there was no need for a "test" of insanity such as those we have today, because the nature of trials was very different.

In the twelfth and thirteenth centuries, the king's court established its control over England, and autonomous local courts were replaced by a jury system. But until the fourteenth century, the jury was merely a fact-finding body without authority to make decisions on its own. Twelve good men and true, the countrymen and acquaintances of the accused, the jurors presented the facts to the king's justices, who reached a verdict. By the fifteenth century the jury became a trier of fact rather than a fact finder, and it was they who entered the verdict, though neither justices nor jurors had the right to go beyond the facts and modify that verdict according to extenuating or excusing circumstances. If the defendant had committed the act, they had to convict; if he was insane, or a minor, or had killed in self-defense, they could recommend mercy, but the granting of mercy was the sole province of the king. There was no need for tests of exculpatory insanity because the only criteria for a pardon were those dictated by the king's opinion and conscience.

In the sixteenth century, however, the jury gained the authority not only to weigh the facts and arrive at a verdict, but to enter their own "special verdict" if they thought that particular circumstances negated the guilt of the accused. With so much power in the hands of twelve citizens, there was a danger that juries might run wild with their own uncontrolled sense of justice, and various devices were contrived to keep them within bounds deemed acceptable to the king and his government. "Fact" and "law" emerged as two distinct entities: jurors were entitled to weigh the facts, but a judge would tell them the law stipulating what was or was not a fact in the first place, and whether and how they should weigh it. Insanity, for example, might excuse from guilt, but not just any form of insanity. The king and the justices felt that they had a general notion of how mad a man must be for acquittal, and they did not want to cast national policy on the matter open to the whimsical sympathies of twelve men here and twelve men there. There was, therefore, as an American jurist later remarked, a tendency "for the learned and great judges to bestow their learning very liberally upon the ignorant and degraded jury, by way of instructions."[7]

The instructions that were actually given in courts undoubtedly varied enormously. Most judges then, as now, had very little experience with insanity cases or madmen, and were forced to rely on whatever sources they could find. Unfortunately, many statements originally intended as illustrative arguments rather than exclusive definitions of insanity were adopted in this way by the legal profession and transformed through repetition into standardized rules. Thus Bracton had commented, in connection with civil cases of lunacy, that a madman "lacks mind and reason, and is not much removed from a brute," and though this was never meant as a restrictive test of insanity, so great was Bracton's authority that his casual association of madmen with beasts would occasionally lead courts to maintain that nothing short of bestial, slavering mania could entitle a lunatic to acquittal. Similarly, the early-sixteenth-century judge Sir Anthony Fitzherbert described an idiot as "such a person who cannot account or number twenty pence, nor can tell who was his father or mother, nor how old he is, etc."[8] The "twenty pence test," which was merely an example, and pertained to idiots rather than lunatics, was nonetheless sometimes used as a strict diagnostic criterion in civil lunacy cases and even cited with approval at criminal trials.

The most common definition, however, was the abstract "knowledge of good and evil" test. In the Old Testament story of creation it was the fruit of the tree of knowledge of good and evil that caused man's expulsion from blissful innocence— that condemned him to a mortal life of misery, and yet gave him the godlike ability and necessity to discern good from evil, right from wrong. Drawn from the roots both of Christian morality and English jurisprudence, this deceptively simple formulation was given wide circulation in legal handbooks as the most absolute test of insanity. The 1581 *Eirenarcha, or of the Offices of the Justices of Peace*, which was widely used for several decades, mentions the knowledge of good and evil. Dalton's *The Country Justice*, a similar practical manual published thirty-seven years later, offers the advice, "If one that is *'non compos mentis,'* or an ideot, kill a man, this is no felony, for they have not knowledge of Good and Evil, nor can have a felonious intent, nor a will or mind to do harm."[9] The rule seemed quite sound in principle; the difficulties of translating theory into practice would appear only much later.

The seventeenth-century legal commentators Edward Coke and Matthew Hale both recognized the difficulty of defining the range of exculpatory insanity. Coke pointed out that there were not only idiots and the chronically insane, who must be considered irresponsible at all times, but episodic lunatics, who were sometimes utterly mad but who, during "lucid intervals," must be held accountable for their misdeeds. To this difficult category, Hale added those suffering from "partial insanity," where the lunatic had an intact "use of reason" on most subjects, yet was chronically deranged and morbidly preoccupied on others, as with melancholics who are burdened with "excessive fears or griefs." Hale believed that most criminals labor under some degree of partial insanity when they commit their crimes; therefore, though such an affliction might be a clinical explanation, considerations of public safety insisted that it not be admitted as an excuse. For acquittal,

2

THE EARLY ENGLISH
INSANITY TRIALS

The theories of Bracton, Coke, and Hale exerted enormous influence on legal thinking about the insanity defense, but its true development is found in the courtroom, where the statements of counsel and judges set examples and precedents for what would take place at subsequent trials. A sequence of English cases, beginning in 1724 and culminating in 1843 with the trial of Daniel McNaughton, firmly established not only the precise "test" of insanity that the witnesses were told to address and the jurors instructed to consider, but laid a pattern of trial tactics that has changed little since.

In 1724, Edward Arnold was accused of feloniously shooting at and wounding Lord Thomas Onslow, a crime punishable, as were most crimes, by death.[1] Arnold was an odd, unemployed local character who survived by hunting and fishing and through the benevolence of others. A succession of witnesses testified that as a child he would toss red-hot coals in his father's dinner plate, laugh foolishly, speak without meaning, hoot like an owl, or shout "cuckoo!" A former landlady said he lacked the sense to come in from the rain, and once tore up her carpet and stuck bits of it in his ears. On more than one occasion he had threatened suicide or asked his barber to slit his throat. A local publican said that "mad Ned Arnold" had been drinking at her pub not long before and complained that Lord Onslow was in his belly, and the amused drinkers had jokingly offered to accompany Arnold to Onslow's house and tell the lord of the peculiar inconvenience he was causing poor Ned. Arnold at other times claimed that Onslow was the cause of all the wicked devices, tumults, and confusions in the land, and that the lord afflicted him, personally, with bugs, bollies, plagues, and bolleroys. Still, there was no substantial reason for Arnold to accost Lord Onslow as he rode down a lane and shoot him in front of two witnesses, and the defense raised was insanity.

The prosecutor tried to discredit the assertion of insanity in a way that will become familiar: by showing that Arnold was not totally bereft of reason. His friends thought him mad, they said, but they had never tried to shut him away. On the day of the crime he had borrowed a gun, bought shot and powder, test-fired the weapon, and asked a passerby if he had seen Lord Onslow, all of which indicated purpose and design. After firing, Arnold ran away, and while in prison he professed sorrow for what he had done. As the prosecutor remarked, there is no surer sign of guilt than remorse.

The judge's instructions in the case have since been regarded as an example of judicial barbarity, and are grotesquely referred to as the "Wild Beast Test." Judge Tracy told the jurors that if a man was "under the visitation of God" and could not distinguish right from wrong, then he could not be guilty because he would lack wickedness of mind. Lest the jury interpret this too broadly, however, Tracy cautioned them:

> . . . it is not every kind of frantic humour or something unaccountable in a man's actions, that points him out to be such a madman as is to be exempted from punishment; it must be a man that is totally deprived of his understanding and memory, and doth not know what he is

doing, no more than an infant, than a brute, or a wild beast.

After a short deliberation, the jury found Arnold guilty, and he was sentenced to death. The victim, however, was more sympathetic than the law, and on Lord Onslow's intercession Arnold was reprieved, and spent the remaining three decades of his life in jail.

In 1760 Lawrence, Earl Ferrers,[2] shot and killed his steward, for whom he had developed a pathological hatred. There was no doubt of his guilt, nor that he had laid careful plans for the deed. As the steward lay dying, Ferrers told everyone who would listen that he had fully intended to commit murder, and he refused to let the wounded man be removed from his house, saying that he wanted to "plague the rascal" during his last hours. When a band of armed villagers came to arrest him, the earl clapped his hands and exclaimed, "I shot a villain and a scoundrel. I glory in his death."

In those times, the privilege of trial by one's peers was quite literally applied to nobility, so that a peer indicted for treason or a felony was tried before the House of Lords. The accused, in addition, was obliged to conduct his own defense, which in this case proved a serious disadvantage since the defense raised, apparently at his family's insistence, was one of insanity. Except for the craziness of proceedings in which counsel referred to the defendant variously as "lord Ferrers," "my lord," and "me," it was a strain to believe insanity present when it was the alleged lunatic himself who carefully questioned witnesses on his frequent tenacious wrongheaded-ness in business deals, fits of abnormal, groundless rage, and the possible taint of hereditary insanity.

It was certain that Lord Ferrers was a peculiar and not altogether rational man prone to unreasonable fears and sus-picions, but the Solicitor General who prosecuted wondered aloud whether Ferrers' behavior in this instance was not more clearly and simply the product of "a bad heart and a vicious mind" than of lunacy. "My lords," he appealed to the House, "in some sense, every crime proceeds from insanity. All cruelty, all brutality, all revenge, all injustice, is insanity. There were philosophers, in ancient times, who held this opinion, as a strict maxim of their sect; and, my lords, this opinion is right in philosophy, but dangerous in judicature."

The Lords were instructed on insanity according to a strict reading of Hale: that one might be acquitted in the case of a total permanent want of reason or a total temporary want, but not otherwise. If there was a partial degree of insanity mingled with a degree of reason "sufficient to have restrained those passions, which produced the crime; if there be thought and design; a faculty to distinguish the nature of actions; to discern the difference between moral good and evil; then, upon the fact of the offense proved, the judgment of the law must take place."

Lord Ferrers was convicted. To his plea for commutation of the death sentence, the Lord High Steward replied that the present, terrestrial tribunal could offer him no respite, but that perhaps he might find solace in the thought that "you are soon to appear before an Almighty Judge, whose unfathomable wisdom is able, by means incomprehensible to our narrow capacities, to reconcile justice with mercy."

In May 1800 James Hadfield fired a pistol at King George III as the monarch entered the royal box at the Drury Lane Theatre, and when tried on the capital charge of treason he raised a defense of insanity.[3] In typical prosecutorial fashion, the Attorney General tried to combat this defense by showing that the defendant was not wholly without reason, and had acted with intelligent purpose. He mentioned as proof the fact that Hadfield had formed the intention of going to the theater, "had that use of his understanding which enabled him to procure the admission," could choose a seat with a clear view of the royal box, and had cleverly managed to stand on his seat so that he could shoot above the heads of the other spectators, to aim his gun, and to pull the trigger. If this type of purpose was proof of sane reasoning, one might say that in the Attorney General's view, the very fact of *doing* an act proved one's responsibility for it, and one could be mentally innocent only of those things that one could never contrive to achieve in the first place.

Hadfield's defense counsel, Thomas Erskine, a brilliant orator and later the Lord Chancellor, took exception to the standard tests of insanity and said he doubted that Coke and Hale's reference to such things as a "total deprivation of memory" could have been intended in a literal sense. It was rare, indeed, that one found insane persons so totally deranged that they did not know their own name, nor the road to their home, nor recognize their family, and these people, when they do exist, are scarcely fit to commit crimes. Except in the total idiot, he said with fine poetic flair, "reason is not driven from her seat, but distraction sits down upon it along with her, holds her, trembling, upon it, and frightens her from her propriety."

The real test of insanity, he said, should not be the ability to think, or the mere awareness of right and wrong, but rather the presence or absence of *delusion*. A man might be perfectly conversant on the issue of moral and legal rectitude, yet apply these standards incorrectly to his own behavior because of a fundamental flaw in his perception of things. "Such persons often reason with a subtlety which puts in the shade the ordinary conceptions of mankind: their conclusions are just, and frequently profound; but the *premises from which they reason*, **WHEN WITHIN THE RANGE OF THE MALADY**, are uniformly false:—not false from any defect of knowledge or judgment; but, because a delusive image, the inseparable companion of real insanity, is thrust upon the subjugated understanding, incapable of resistance, because unconscious of attack."

To illustrate the subtlety of madness, Erskine mentioned the case of a madman named Wood who had sued an asylum keeper for false imprisonment. The keeper's counsel failed abysmally to elicit the slightest suggestion of lunacy from the perfectly lucid Wood until a doctor suggested that he ask about the princess and the cherry juice. Wood said there was nothing in all that: everyone knew he had been imprisoned in a high tower and denied the use of ink, so that he had to write his letters in cherry juice and throw them into the river that ran around the tower, where the princess picked them up in her boat. This example was striking, but Erskine neglected to mention that it bore no necessary relationship to the question of criminal responsibility: had Wood murdered someone, his closely circumscribed delusion about princesses and cherry juice would not, alone, have negated his blame for the act.

Erskine's splendid argument in favor of delusion as a test was, in fact, demanded by the peculiar exigencies of Hadfield's case. He had at all costs to cast doubt upon the right-wrong test, since it was precisely because Hadfield did know the difference between right and wrong and did appreciate the illegality and enormity of his crime that he had fired at King George. James Hadfield was a former soldier who had served valiantly in the French Revolutionary Wars. In 1794 he had been severely wounded in battle. Two sword blows penetrated his skull to the brain, two more—if Erskine can be believed— all but severed his head from his body, so that the gallant Hadfield fought on with his head dangling onto his chest. His hand was chopped to the bone, he was stabbed through the body with a bayonet, and his comrades finally abandoned him for dead. Erskine invited the jurors to inspect the mutilated defendant, and the piteous spectacle was probably at least as persuasive as any of the testimony.

Hadfield's lunacy dated from the time of his wounds. While recovering, he believed himself to be King George, and would stand before a hospital mirror, stroking his face and head, searching, he said, for his golden crown. In subsequent years, he had raving fits so uncontrollable that his family had to lock him in his room or lash him to his bed. His delusion changed, and he claimed he had spoken with God or Christ, or at other times that he was God or Christ. Shortly before the crime he conceived the notion that mankind was doomed to disaster, and that the only thing that could avert this fate was his martyrdom. He did not wish to commit suicide, which was a sin, nor did he wish to harm King George, whom he admired; since attempted regicide was a capital offense, he had fired close to the king, feigning an attempt on the royal person, as a means to his own demise.

Twelve witnesses presented the woeful history of James Hadfield, and finally Chief Justice Kenyon interrupted to ask Erskine whether he was nearly through. Erskine replied that he had twenty more witnesses, which was far more than anyone needed or wanted to hear, whatever insanity test might be used, and the Attorney General consented to Kenyon's suggestion that the case be stopped. The jury was advised to enter a verdict of not guilty, and it was further suggested, for the sake of posterity, that the foreman append the reason for this acquittal: "he being under the influence of Insanity at the time the act was committed."

Until this time, acquitted lunatics had been disposed of in whatever way seemed appropriate to the court in light of the nature of the defendant and of his crime. Some of them were sent to jail. Others were released to the custody of their family, particularly if the family was responsible and wealthy and had a large country house with secure bolts on the doors. Five years earlier a Scottish baronet, Sir Archibald Kinloch, had been acquitted of fratricide by reason of insanity and promptly released to his family, which posted £10,000 surety guaranteeing to have him confined in "sure and safe custody, during all the days of his life."[4] None of this, however, was altogether legal, since there was no statute giving courts the authority thus to dispose of a man who had been adjudicated innocent of any crime.

The prominence of Hadfield's case led to the correction of this situation. A month after the trial the king gave the Royal Assent to an "Act for the safe Custody of Insane Persons charged with Offenses,"[5] stipulating that henceforth defendants found not guilty by reason of insanity must be held "in such place and in such manner as to his Majesty shall seem fit." Just where and how this should be done was not immediately determined, and would remain a problem for some time.

James Hadfield himself was sent to Bethlem Hospital, but he periodically returned to the public eye. In 1802 it was falsely rumored that he had murdered a fellow inmate, and several years later he escaped from the hospital and reached Dover before being recaptured. In 1840 an Attorney General visited the famous criminal lunatic and reported that he "talked very rationally upon the topics of the day; but he continued at times subject to strong delusion, and it would have been very unsafe to have discharged him from custody."[6] The following year, at age sixty-nine, Hadfield died in Bedlam.

That John Bellingham was mentally ill seems quite certain; whether or not he was legally insane was impossible to tell, since scarcely any evidence was permitted at his trial while justice rushed him to the gallows.

Bellingham was an Englishman who had failed at a number of business ventures, gone to Russia in hopes of making his fortune in trade, and ended up jailed there as a debtor in 1805. He applied to the British ambassador for help, claiming that the charges against him were false, but after a perfunctory inquiry, that official said he was unable to intervene in a question of Russian domestic affairs. Bellingham was held in prison for five years, and upon his release he returned to England determined to obtain redress. He felt not only that he had suffered grievous personal and financial loss, but that his lamentable treatment constituted a Russian insult to the English people as a whole. He felt that the English government owed him some form of compensation, since it was the ambassador's neglectful attitude that was responsible for his distress.

In the six months before his crime, Bellingham petitioned every government figure and agency he could think of. None of the officials believed that he had a valid claim, but in typical bureaucratic style, each referred him elsewhere, and yet elsewhere, in a dizzying whirl of rejected petitions. Finally, through some vague logic of his own, Bellingham decided upon assassination as the only solution to his problems, and on May 11, 1812, he stationed himself in the lobby of the House of Parliament, and when Prime Minister Spencer Perceval entered, shot him dead. "I admit the fact," he calmly admitted soon afterwards, "but wish, with permission, to state something in my justification. I have been denied the redress of my grievances by Government; I have been ill-treated. . . . I am a most unfortunate man, and feel here (placing his hand on his breast) sufficient justification for what I have done."[7]

The crime was committed on Monday, May 11; Bellingham's trial began and ended on Friday, May 15. He entered the courtroom as calmly as he would mount the scaffold the following week. His lawyer promptly asked for a postponement, since he had had only two days to prepare, and was unable to contact many witnesses who could testify to Bellingham's insanity, though he had obtained affidavits from others. He had written to two eminent medical men, but one could not attend that day, and the other had not yet replied.

The Attorney General accused defense counsel of fishing for sympathy. The affidavits, he claimed, were "flimsy contrivances," and "these persons, who swore the affidavits, must have been selected with the view to impose a false belief upon the Court, and to baffle for a time the dread purposes of justice." The judge, Sir James Mansfield, agreed that no further time should be allowed because it was not a question of introducing material facts relevant to the case. He went on to say, from the judicial bench itself, that "[e]very word in the affidavits might be perfectly true; at the same time that it was as clear as daylight, that at the time of the commission of this deed he was in a sound state of mind."[8]

The Attorney General eulogized Spencer Perceval: spoke of his widow and children, the loss to the country, the life cut short for nothing more than one man's "resentment." He outlined Bellingham's plans to commit the foul deed: how he had special pockets sewn in his coat to hold his pistols, how he ascertained the Prime Minister's usual time of arrival at the House, how he positioned himself in the lobby. The intent was regrettably clear. As for his insanity, the Attorney General said that Bellingham had always conducted his own business affairs, and pointed out that if, on the day of the crime, Almighty God had arrested his hand and Bellingham had chosen to write a will or a contract instead, no court would have deemed it invalid. No one had ever tried to commit him. "Are we to conclude, in fact, the prisoner to be mad, [simply] because he has done an act of madness? If so, Gentlemen, this very atrocious and extraordinarily wicked act carries with it its own defence; and we may do what we please against the justice of the country, provided our conduct be sufficiently daring, and boasts an atrocity beyond the wickedness of common life."[9]

Defense counsel was left with little to say. Bellingham himself asked permission to address the court. He thanked his lawyer for his zealous and well-intended efforts, but was even more grateful to the Attorney General for refuting the insanity defense. It would not serve his purpose to be found insane, since this might damage his chances of justifying his claims against the government. He regretted the fate of Prime Minister

Perceval sincerely, but did not feel personally responsible. Circumstances had made the death necessary, and he was no more than the instrument of ineluctable events. Bellingham then spent more than an hour telling the court about his persecution in Russia and the truly extraordinary steps he had taken to find satisfaction of his claims.

Judge Mansfield instructed the jury that "no circumstances of injury, however aggravated, could warrant any man for taking the law into his own hands, and taking away the life of an individual. Neither could the plea of insanity be of any avail in such a case, unless it could be proved that the prisoner, at the time he committed the act, was so far deranged in his mind, as not to be capable of judging between right and wrong."[10] The jury retired briefly, and returned with a verdict of guilty. As Bellingham stood cheerfully on the gallows three days later, he was asked if he had any last words, but was cut short when he began speaking of Russia.

As Queen Victoria and Prince Albert rode in their carriage on June 10, 1840, a man by the roadside turned to them and nodded, then pulled a pair of pistols and fired two shots, both of which missed. Passersby seized the wrong man, but the real culprit, Edward Oxford,[11] stepped up to them and said, "It was me, I did it, I surrender myself." When his apartment was searched, police found correspondence from a revolutionary group called "Young England," detailing the organization's uniforms, weaponry, false names, and disguises, though no indication of what purpose the group served. It was later shown that the documents were all in Oxford's hand, and that the group existed only in his mind.

Oxford was charged with high treason and pleaded not guilty, implicitly by reason of insanity. The Attorney General cautioned the jury that though insanity was a quite proper defense in its place, mere weakness of intellect, eccentricity, or violent tendencies did not justify such a verdict. Oxford

19

had bought a pair of pistols and a powder flask a month before the crime, and practiced shooting at a target range. A week prior to the assassination attempt he purchased more copper caps and bullets to put into his weapons. Therefore, the prosecutor's reasoning went, Edward Oxford had rational, evil intent.

The defense gave evidence of Oxford's tainted heredity. His grandfather had gone mad and spent the last years of his life in a madhouse, where he claimed to be either the Pope or St. Paul. Oxford's mother testified that her former husband, Edward's father, had also been mad: he sometimes burned bank notes and had often threatened suicide. He made hideous grimaces at her during her pregnancy, jumped about like a baboon, once knocked her down and fractured her head, and when she was nursing he stabbed her in the breast with a file. Her second child, after Edward, was a confirmed idiot.

Edward Oxford was eighteen years old at the time of the crime, just the age, defense counsel stated, when "the taint of hereditary insanity would be most likely to break out." His mother said he had been troublesome and unsettling from the earliest age: he was prone to inexplicable bouts of weeping, sudden fits of destruction, and alternating periods of gloom and hysterical laughter. At times he was extremely affectionate, at others inhumanly cold. He once punched his mother in the nose, and on another occasion a policeman brought him home after he jumped up behind a pregnant woman's carriage and frightened her with a loud noise; at neither time did he appear conscious of having done any wrong.

Oxford was briefly employed at the Shepherd and Flock public house, where his performance was unsatisfactory. He neglected his duties and sat by himself, weeping into his apron or laughing outrageously. "I have asked him why he was laughing," testified a policeman who knew him; "he said, 'The old women drank so much gin, it would make any one laugh'; I said, 'There are no old women here now'; he said, 'No, there is not.' " Once a customer came in for stout, and the publican asked Oxford to bottle it. Oxford put bottles upside down in a basket, stuck a funnel among them, and doused stout all over the basket.

Five physicians were called at Oxford's trial, some of them specializing in mental disorders, one of them a coroner. All agreed he was of unsound mind, though their precise testimony is not detailed in the record.

Lord Denman, the chief justice, told the jury that the question they must consider was "whether the evidence given proves a disease in the mind as of a person quite incapable of distinguishing right from wrong . . . whether the prisoner was labouring under the species of insanity which satisfies you that he was quite unaware of the nature, character, and consequences of the act he was committing, or, in other words, whether he was under the influence of a diseased mind, and was really unconscious at the time he was committing the act, that it was a crime."

The jury found Oxford guilty of discharging two pistols, and insane, but they were unable to decide whether or not his weapons had been loaded, since no slugs were ever found. Chief Justice Denman advised them to make up their minds, and while the jurors were out, members of the court discussed what should be done with the prisoner. The Attorney General said that under the 1800 act the court must order all persons found not guilty of a crime by reason of insanity to be kept in custody at His Majesty's Pleasure. Others of the court, anticipating an objection that would continue to be heard, more stridently, over a century later, remarked that it seemed odd that an acquitted lunatic could be entrusted to the mercy of the crown quite possibly for life, when a conviction on the same charge, such as discharging a pistol, would have earned him no more than six months in prison. The Attorney General replied that a prisoner raised the insanity defense at his own risk, and must take the consequences.

The jury circumvented its difficulty with the pistols by dropping the initial conviction and finding Oxford simply not guilty by reason of insanity: it was not really clear what it was that he was not guilty of. He was promptly committed to the Bethlem Asylum where, as some had feared, he spent a very long time. The first entry in his medical file there does not even appear until fourteen years later, when it was noted that he always "conducted himself with great propriety," cooperated fully, and devoted his spare time to instructive reading and study. He had, in fact, taught himself French, German, Italian, Spanish, Latin, and Greek, and was beginning to study the violin. He excelled at everything he tried, including knitting and housepainting, and was the asylum chess and checker champion. "With regard to his crime he now laments the act, which probably originated in a feeling of excessive vanity and a desire to become notorious if he could not be celebrated."[12]

Despite such intelligence, industry, and penitence, Oxford would remain at Bethlem for ten years more, and in 1864 was among the first patients transferred to the new Broadmoor Criminal Lunatic Asylum. Finally, however, and rather uniquely, in 1867 the Home Secretary ordered Oxford released on the condition that he leave the United Kingdom at once and never return. Oxford boarded a ship for Melbourne, and was not heard of again.[13]

3

THE TRIAL OF
DANIEL McNAUGHTON

This sequence of cases does not show any particular progression in the insanity defense. The type of instructions varied widely, though all were intended to convey the basic notion that insanity deserved an acquittal if it was truly a serious form of insanity and not mere viciousness or oddity. It is not at all clear how the jurors applied these tests to the defendant, though it may be more than coincidence that, with the exception of Edward Arnold, there was a tendency to convict defendants who succeeded in killing their victims, while acquitting the ones who failed. In 1843 the situation would change, and one firm rule was laid down.

On January 20, 1843, Edward Drummond, the very popular private secretary to the Tory Prime Minister, Sir Robert Peel, was walking near Charing Cross on the way from his banking house to his home when a man stepped behind him, pulled a pistol from the left breast of his coat, and shot Drummond in the back at point-blank range. The assassin calmly returned the weapon to its place, and began drawing another pistol, but was restrained by a nearby policeman, who grabbed his arm and knocked him to the ground.

On the way to the police station, the prisoner muttered that "he" or "she"—the arresting officer was not sure which—

"shall not break my peace of mind any longer." A search of the man's pockets produced, along with spare bullets, some money, and the usual miscellaneous jumble, a slip of paper bearing an address and the name "Daniel McNaughton."*

Drummond died of his wound five days after the shooting, and McNaughton's murder trial[3] began at the Old Bailey on March 3. A plea of insanity was laboriously drawn from the

---

* There has been great debate over the spelling of McNaughton's name, which in the United States is most commonly spelled "M'Naghten." In 1952, after the *Times* of London printed an article referring to "M'Naughten," U.S. Supreme Court Justice Felix Frankfurter wrote a letter to the editor asking whether this was not an error, given that Clark & Finnelly—the authoritative report of the case—gave "M'Naghten." *Times* editor Sir William J. Haley replied that the writer of the article had undertaken some research and found the following variant spellings:

1. The original Gaelic—Mhicneachdain
2. The lunatic himself, signing a letter produced at the trial (and reported in the *Times* at the time)—M'Naughten
3. The State Trials—Macnaughton
4. Clark and Finnelly—M'Naghten
5. Archbold, 1938 edition—Macnaughton
   1927 edition—Macnaughten
   Index—Macnaghten
6. Stephen, earlier editions—Macnaughten
   later editions—Macnaghten
7. Halsbury, earlier editions—M'Naughton
   later editions—M'Naughton
8. Select Committee on Capital Punishment, 1930—McNaughten, and several other spellings
9. Encyclopaedia Britannica—different spellings in different articles
10. Royal Commission on Capital Punishment, 1949, instructed by its chairman, Sir Ernest Gowers—M'Naghten

Sir William Haley, in conclusion, said that the *Times* had chosen to use the man's own version of his name; Justice Frankfurter deferred to the weighty authority of the *Times*, but nonetheless jokingly inquired, "To what extent is a lunatic's spelling even of his own name to be deemed an authority?"[1]

Bernard Diamond[2] observes that, in spite of the *Times*, the sole specimen of McNaughton's own signature looks like "McNaughton" rather than "M'Naughton." For that matter, he states, it *really* looks like "McNaughtun," but this is about the only spelling that no one will accept on any authority. Diamond also points out that the apostrophe in "M'Naghten" is not properly an apostrophe at all, but a reversed apostrophe or inverted comma used by printers who lacked a small *c* that could be placed above the line. As type fonts improved, most M' names have become Mc.

"McNaughton" is the spelling that will be used throughout this book except in quotations, where the original author's orthography shall be respected.

defendant. Solicitor General Sir William Webb Follett, leading the prosecution for the crown, attacked the defense with the familiar old routine:

> This defence is a difficult one at all times; for while, on the one hand, everyone must be anxious that an unconscious being should not suffer, on the other hand, the public safety requires that this defence should not be too readily listened to. . . . The whole question will turn upon this: if you believe the prisoner at the bar at the time he committed this act was not a responsible agent; if you believe that when he fired the pistol he was incapable of distinguishing between right and wrong; if you believe that he was under the influence and control of some disease of the mind which prevented him from being conscious that he was committing a crime; if you believe that he did not know he was violating the law both of God and man; then, undoubtedly, he is entitled to your acquittal. But it is my duty . . . to tell you that nothing short of that will excuse him upon the principle of English law.

The prosecution sought to prove sanity by demonstrating that the prisoner had behaved rationally—that if a sane man had chosen to murder Mr. Drummond, he might have gone about it in just the same manner. McNaughton had, in fact, actually intended to shoot Sir Robert Peel, but his mistake was understandable, since the two men resembled one another, and Drummond lived at the Prime Minister's residence and often rode in his employer's carriage.

McNaughton had spent about two weeks loitering on steps and in doorways around Whitehall, where he finally committed the murder. This implied forethought and planning. When asked what he was doing there, he invented plausible lies, such as that he was waiting for someone, or that he was a policeman. Thus he was sane enough to tell falsehoods, and recognized the need for averting suspicion. A witness to the shooting said that McNaughton drew and cocked his pistol quickly, but that "it was a very cool, deliberate act." The Solicitor General said nothing of the defendant's lack of plans for escape, he having opened fire on a busy street in broad daylight, with a policeman nearly at his elbow.

McNaughton's landlady and six other witnesses said they had never noticed signs of mental abnormality in him: he had comported himself in a reasonable manner, and conducted intelligent business transactions. A man who had known him for years said that "he appeared to be a particularly mild and inoffensive person," and a Glasgow surgeon whose medical lectures McNaughton once attended had found that, though his pupil was not well educated, he appeared to understand the lectures and had manifested no signs of insanity during them.

The defense countered the prosecution's strict definition of exculpatory insanity with a quotation from Roscoe's *Criminal Evidence* indicating that the issue could be much more subtle than a simple question of intellectual awareness of right and wrong:

Although a prisoner understands perfectly the distinction between right and wrong, yet if he labours, as is generally the case, under an illusion and deception in his own particular case, and is thereby incapable of applying it correctly to his own conduct, he is in that state of mental aberration which renders him not criminally answerable for his actions. For example, a mad person may be perfectly aware that murder is a crime, and will admit it, if pressed on the subject; still he may conceive that the homicide he has committed was nowise blamable, because the deceased had engaged in a conspiracy, with others, against his own life, or was his mortal enemy, who had wounded him in his dearest interests, or was the devil incarnate, whom it was the duty of every good Christian to meet with weapons of carnal warfare.

As applied to McNaughton this seemed to be true, since though he was intelligent and lucid in some respects, there was strong evidence that he had suffered from paranoid delusions for many years. McNaughton was the natural son of a Glasgow woodturner, and had followed his father's profession. During seven years of apprenticeship he had been reliable, industrious, and temperate in his habits, but as he reached manhood and embarked on his own he grew increasingly strange and distant. About two years before the crime, McNaughton suddenly sold the business he had run for five years, and his behavior became downright alarming. He told his father that spies were following him day and night, and that though they never said anything they laughed at him, or shook their fists or sticks, and one threw straws in his face to indicate that they meant to reduce him to beggary.

McNaughton told the journeyman who purchased his business that spies prevented him from obtaining work. He appealed to various government officials, who could scarcely follow his rambling account of persecution and suggested that rather than coming to the government he should seek out a medical specialist. Before settling on the Tories as his antagonists, he blamed other political parties, Catholic priests, and the Jesuits. A fellow lodger said that McNaughton sometimes got up in the middle of the night and walked about undressed for an hour or more muttering "By Jove" and "My God." Still, he seemed harmless and kind, loved to watch children at play because "he liked to see their innocence," and carried bread to feed the birds.

Some months before the crime, McNaughton was evicted from his lodging house after other boarders objected to his wild moans and mutterings. He complained that the spies followed him into his bedroom, so he began sleeping in open fields in the suburbs. He booked passage to France to escape from his persecutors, but as the boat docked at Boulogne, he saw one of the spies peeping at him from behind the watch box on the customhouse quay; realizing that they would follow him to the ends of the earth, he chose not to waste his money fleeing further into Europe, and turned back to England.

One of the witnesses at the trial was the prominent alienist Dr. E. T. Monro, who had examined McNaughton following the crime, and gave the following account of the defendant's mental state:

[T]he prisoner said he was persecuted by a system or crew at Glasgow, Edinburgh, Liverpool, London, and Boulogne. That this crew preceded or followed him wherever he went; that he had no peace of mind, and he was sure it would kill him; that it was grinding of the mind. I asked him if he had availed himself of medical advice? He replied, that physicians could be of no service to him, for if he took a ton of drugs it would be of no service to him; that in Glasgow he observed people in the streets pointing at him, and speaking of him. They said that is the man, he is a murderer and the worst of characters. That everything was done to associate his name with the direst of crimes. He was tossed like a cork on the sea, and that wherever he went, in town or country, on sea or shore, he was perpetually watched and followed. At Edinburgh he saw a man on horseback watching him. That another person there nodded to him, and exclaimed, "That's he"; that he had applied to the authorities of Glasgow for protection and relief. His complaints had been sneered and scould at by Sheriff Bell, who had it in his power to put a stop to the persecution, if he had liked. If he had had a pistol in his possession, he would have shot Sheriff Bell dead as he sat in the court-house; that Mr. Salmond, the procurator-fiscal, Mr. Sheriff Bell, Sheriff Alison, and Sir R. Peel might have put a stop to this system of persecution if they would; that on coming out of the court-house he had seen a man frowning at him, with a bundle of straw under his arm; that he knew well enough

28

what was meant; that everything was done by signs; that he was represented to be under a delusion; that the straw denoted that he should lie upon straw in an asylum; that whilst on board the steamboat on his way from Glasgow to Liverpool, he was watched, eyed, and examined closely by persons coming near him; that they had followed him to Boulogne on two occasions; they would never allow him to learn French, and wanted to murder him—he was afraid of going out after dark, for fear of assassination—that individuals were made to appear before him, like those he had seen at Glasgow. He mentioned having applied to Mr. A. Johnston, M.P. for Kilmarnock, for protection; Mr. Johnston had told him that he (the prisoner) was labouring under a delusion, but that he was sure he was not. That he had seen paragraphs in the *Times* newspaper containing allusions which he was satisfied were directed at him; he had seen articles also in the *Glasgow Herald,* beastly and atrocious, insinuating things untrue and insufferable of him; that on one or two occasions something pernicious had been put into his food; that he had studied anatomy to obtain peace of mind, but he had not found it. That he imagined the person at whom he fired at Charing Cross to be one of the crew—a part of the system that was destroying his health. . . . He observed that when he saw the person at Charing Cross at whom he fired, every feeling of suffering which he had endured for months and years rose up at once in his mind, and that he conceived that he should obtain peace by killing him.

Two more physicians testified and agreed with Monro that McNaughton was insane. Curiously, neither of them had examined the defendant; they had been present during the trial as spectators, and based their conclusions on the testimony they heard and their observations of the prisoner in the box. This very ignorance, however, carried particular weight, and after they had spoken, Chief Justice Nicholas Tindal said: "We feel the evidence, especially that of the last two medical gentlemen who have been examined, and who are strangers to both sides and only observers of the case, to be very strong, and sufficient to induce my learned brothers and myself to stop the case." The Solicitor General agreed to this decision, the trial was halted, and Daniel McNaughton, declared insane, was committed to an insane asylum.

Though the prosecution, defense, and court were content with the verdict, this could not be said of the population at large. An irate citizen submitted a poem to the *Times* entitled "On a Late Acquittal," which read in part:

> Ye people of England exult and be glad
> For ye're now at the will of the merciless mad.
> Why say ye that but three authorities reign
> Crown, Commons, and Lords?—You omit the insane.
> They're a privileged class whom no statute controls,
> And their murderous charter exists in their souls.
> Do they wish to spill blood—they have only to play
> A few pranks—get asylum'd a month and a day
> Then Heigh! to escape from the mad doctor's keys
> And to pistol or stab whomsoever they please.[4]

Queen Victoria herself strongly protested the decision in a letter to McNaughton's intended victim, Sir Robert Peel:

> The law may be perfect, but how is [it] that whenever a case for its application arises, it proves to be of no avail? We have seen the trials of Oxford and MacNaghten conducted by the ablest lawyers of the day . . . , and *they allow* and *advise* the Jury to pronounce the verdict of *Not Guilty* on account of *Insanity*,—whilst *everybody* is morally *convinced* that both malefactors were perfectly conscious and aware of what they did! It appears from this, that the force of the law is entirely put into the judge's hands, and that it depends merely upon his charge whether the law is to be applied or

not. Could not the Legislature lay down that rule which the
Lord Chancellor does in his paper, and which Chief Justice
Mansfield did in the case of Bellingham; and why could not
the judges be *bound* to interpret the law in *this* and *no
other* sense in their charges to the juries?[5]

In a more lighthearted moment the Queen is said to have
remarked that she "did not believe that anyone could be
insane who wanted to murder a Conservative Prime Minister."

The matter was immediately discussed in Parliament, members of both Houses calling for more stringent legislation. On
March 13, Lord Chancellor Lyndhurst made a long discourse
to the House of Lords and proposed a resolution to the
debates. He cited the judges' instructions in the Bellingham,
Hadfield, and Oxford cases, and several other legal authorities,
all of which, with the exception of Hadfield, mentioned the
knowledge of right and wrong, or of good and evil, as the
pivotal question in the determination of criminal responsibility.
He approved of these previous decisions, and cautioned the
Lords against hasty attempts to change the procedure. "I say,
to attempt to define upon a subject with which we are as yet
only partially acquainted would be difficult and dangerous.
Let us leave the general law as it stands, and let the judges,
before whom prisoners are arraigned and tried, apply the
particular facts to the law so laid down."[6] The problem that
faced them, he said, was that though the prevailing laws were
just, no one was quite certain exactly what they *were*, and he
proposed to summon her majesty's judges before the House
to have them inform the Lords, once and for all, what form
the insanity test should take in the future.

Lord Brougham concurred in this recommendation: judges
could not continue to instruct juries interchangeably in terms
of "capable of knowing right from wrong," "capable of distinguishing good from evil," and a half-dozen other formulations.
A man might know right from wrong without being able to

distinguish good from evil. Accountability to a human tribunal was quite a different thing from one's moral accountability to his Maker, since the Deity, in His infinite mercy, might forgive some men of weakly constituted mind whom her majesty's courts, with the more pragmatic ambition of deterring others, should hold responsible. Lord Brougham was not at all sure that juries knew right from wrong in the *legally* intended sense, and he felt sure that the wanton use of words such as wicked, improper, blamable, proper, right, wrong, good, and evil must sometimes perplex the judges, and bewilder the experts themselves. Consequently, he agreed that the judges should be called "in order that they might give an answer, not merely to the general question, what do you mean by right and wrong, and the capacity of distinguishing between them, but to half a dozen other questions which must succeed it."[7]

Fifteen judges were summoned to the House of Lords on May 26, 1843, and asked five questions, which they returned to answer in June. Lord Chief Justice Tindal, who had presided over McNaughton's trial, read the majority opinion of fourteen judges. The questions were limited in scope, and did not, as Lord Brougham recommended, probe far beyond the mere verbal formulation. One of them simply asked whether medical men who had not examined the defendant should be permitted to testify, to which the judges said they should not.

As to the specific test to be applied by the jury, the judges replied:

> [T]he jurors ought to be told in all cases that every man is to be presumed sane, and to possess a sufficient degree of reason to be responsible for his crimes, until the contrary be proved to their satisfaction; and that TO ESTABLISH A DEFENCE ON THE GROUND OF INSANITY, IT MUST BE CLEARLY PROVED THAT, AT THE TIME OF THE COMMITTING OF THE ACT, THE PARTY ACCUSED WAS LABOURING UNDER SUCH A

DEFECT OF REASON, FROM DISEASE OF THE MIND, AS NOT TO
KNOW THE NATURE AND QUALITY OF THE ACT HE WAS DOING;
OR IF HE DID KNOW IT, THAT HE DID NOT KNOW THAT HE
WAS DOING WHAT WAS WRONG.

One of the most urgent concerns of the Lords had been the
perennially troublesome issue of partial insanity. McNaughton,
Oxford, and most of the difficult cases seemed to fit into this
category mentioned by Coke and Hale. The claim was made
that they were insane even though they were clearly deranged
on a few topics at most, while they otherwise conducted
themselves with comparative normalcy. The judges said that,
assuming a person who "labours under such partial delusion
only, and is not in other respects insane, we think he must be
considered in the same situation as to responsibility as if the
facts with respect to which the delusion exists were real. For
example, if under the influence of his delusion he supposes
another man to be in the act of attempting to take away his
life, and he kills that man, as he supposes, in self-defence, he
would be exempt from punishment. If his delusion was that
the deceased had inflicted injury to his character and fortune,
and he killed him in revenge for such supposed injury, he
would be liable to punishment." In other words, when faced
with a partially insane defendant, the court must adjourn from
the real world, reconvene within the lunatic's delusion, and
decree that the law of England extends to this crazy realm.
McNaughton himself, under the rules which now bear some
variant of his name, would probably not have been acquitted,
since he had not killed in self-defense.

In a lone dissenting opinion, Justice Maule objected that
the decision was far too vague, largely because the questions
themselves were not asked in reference to any particular case
or any particular purpose, and attempted to cover a topic as
variable as human nature with some cursory, abstract formula.
Most of all he objected "from a fear, of which I cannot divest

myself, that as these questions relate to matters of criminal law of great importance and frequent occurrence, the answers to them by the judges may embarrass the administration of justice when they are cited in criminal trials." Concerning the issue of partial delusion in particular, a very intricate problem, Justice Maule felt that "it would require, in order to answer it, a solution of all questions of law which could arise on the circumstances stated in the question, either by explicitly stating and answering such questions, or by stating some principles or rules which would suffice for the solution."

Justice Maule confessed that he himself was unable to foresee and pass judgment upon every possible situation or to propose an ideal, universally applicable formula. Justice Maule did not believe that anyone could.

The central figure in the case, meanwhile, retired to the obscurity of Bethlem Hospital. His original diagnosis was "monomania." Today he would probably be classed as a paranoid schizophrenic. A March 1854 hospital report states:

> [McNaughton] is a man of so retiring a disposition and so averse to conversation or notice of any kind that it is very difficult even for his attendant to glean from him any information as to his state of mind or the character of his delusions, but one point has been made out that he imagines he is the subject of annoyance from some real or fanciful being or beings; but more than this is not known, for he studiously avoids entering into the subject with any one. If a stranger walks through the Gallery he at once hides in the water closet or in a bedroom and at other times he chooses some darkish corner where he reads or knits. . . . He has refused food and been fed with the stomach pump.[8]

McNaughton was transferred to the Broadmoor Criminal Lunatic Asylum in March 1864, and he died there on May 3, 1865, aged fifty-two, of "anaemia, brain disease and gradual failure of heart's action." No stone marks Daniel McNaughton's grave, and its location on the hospital grounds has now been forgotten.

McNaughton's name, on the other hand, had not been forgotten, but grew better known with each passing year. Succinctly formulated, and approved by the House of Lords, the "McNaughton Rule" carried an authoritative weight that none of the previous instructions had, and by the end of the nineteenth century it had been adopted as law not only in England and throughout the British Empire, but in almost every American state. It is curious, and somewhat unfortunate, that this binding precedent should have been set precisely at a time when the underlying assumptions of the right-wrong rule were the objects of scrutiny and attack.

4

PSYCHIATRY
AND THE LAW

Until a few decades into the nineteenth century, medical testimony was a comparative rarity at insanity trials. No physician testified about Edward Arnold: publicans and landladies said that he had lords in his belly and stuck carpeting into his ears. At Bellingham's trial the judge thought medical opinion of insufficient importance to warrant delaying the proceedings for its sake. During one not atypical American case, dated 1816, the only evidence of the defendant's mental state was the disarmingly straightforward assertion by defense counsel himself:

> John A. Graham, of counsel for the prisoner, said that the prisoner was an idiot. Although the jury had no positive testimony on that head, yet he contended there was ocular demonstration of the fact by inspection.... On the first head, the counsel informed the jury that he possessed a knowledge of physiognomy; and that madness itself was stamped on every lineament of the prisoner's countenance, by the hand of nature. I do aver, said he, that every glance of that vacant, staring eye, every movement of that head— nay, his whole exterior, indicates downright madness.[1]

Even when physicians did testify in criminal cases they had

legatees, whether he understood the terms of a contract and appeared able to exercise due care in transactions, and whether or not he knew that his act was wrong, and thus possessed the "guilty mind" or *mens rea* that society has chosen to punish.

By the early nineteenth century, however, a radical change was taking place in the nascent field of psychiatry. New theories of humane treatment replaced the old leech and purge cures, and the favorable results stimulated interest in mental disease. The combination of an optimistic new medical perception and the general nineteenth-century trend toward the institutionalization of social welfare led to the construction of massive state and county asylums, direction of which was regularly assumed by medical men. This, in turn, produced more change yet, since for the first time physicians had the opportunity for prolonged observation of large numbers of patients suffering from a broad spectrum of mental disorders. The monolithic term "insanity" acquired shape and substance. Mental disorders came in different degrees and distinct varieties, and changed over time. The sane mind was not a pure intellect whose ability to "know," "think," and "understand" might be placed higher or lower along a linear scale of cognitive development, but rather a conglomerate of reason and emotion, a complex structure in which disturbances of one part might wreak subtly pervasive alterations in the rest.

Jurists and physicians suddenly found themselves using the same word, "insanity," with different definitions. Medicine eventually abandoned the term altogether except for use in the courtroom, but a certain degree of confusion persists to this day. Some psychiatrists supposed that the law intended to excuse *all* insane defendants from guilt, and was using the absurdly unscientific and lamentably inadequate right-wrong test as a diagnostic device. Asylums, they pointed out, were full of insane people who knew right from wrong: according to one estimate,[2] no more than 2–3 percent of hospitalized lunatics were devoid of free will and discrimination and completely immune to moral influence, and it was only this minority of cases that the McNaughton Rule would identify.

The legal response to this misleading objection was that it did not matter whether or not the right-wrong test was medically accurate, since the question was one not of sickness or health, but of legal responsibility. The law had never meant to excuse all lunatics, but to excuse certain categories of mental and moral innocents, among whom acutely deranged lunatics were one conspicuous example. It was an issue of profound social importance, to be couched in the permanent, abstract principles of law and applied by society's representatives, rather than defined in terms of perpetually changing scientific theories and left to the judgment of one specialized profession. By legal standards, whether or not a defendant had knowingly done wrong seemed a very neat, permanent, and abstract way of determining who should be blamed.

The truth, of course, was at neither extreme, but somewhere between the two. One might wish that the law was a thing of eternal, transcendent perfection, but few believe that it is. As Justice Holmes cautioned, one ought never to treat law as though it were a set of mathematical axioms and corollaries from which theorems for all occasions may be derived. The law must hold a steadier course than the whim of scientific fashion, but it remains a living part of a changing society and, as such, has an obligation not to ignore the progress that science and learning do make. As time went on, it became apparent to some that, even in the law's own terms, the McNaughton Rule might not be an adequate expression of the law's own intent.

The most constructive nineteenth-century dialogue between psychiatry and the law was the collaboration in legal reform undertaken in the late 1860s by Dr. Isaac Ray and Associate Justice Charles Doe of the Supreme Court of New Hampshire. Ray was the most prominent medical authority on the legal aspects of mental disease, and a founder of what would become the American Psychiatric Association. In 1838, when he was a thirty-one-year-old general practitioner in Maine, he had written a remarkable book, *A Treatise on the Medical Jurisprudence of Insanity*, which even today is one of the most lucid and widely read works in the field. It was at the time the most comprehensive treatment of the subject in the English language, and might reasonably be called the first psychiatry text for jurists and first law text for physicians.

Ray described the varieties of mental disorders, and traced the development of both civil and criminal laws concerning the insane. He displayed a persuasive array of cases where people of acute reasoning and quick wit were nonetheless demonstrably insane and prone to irresponsible actions. In the criminal domain he held up appalling examples of some who had been convicted and executed because of the foolish blindness brought about by too close reliance on imperfect verbal formulations.

Some errors were merely shocking, and one wondered how they could happen, such as the case of John Barclay, a young Scot tried at Glasgow in 1833 for murder. He was a congenital idiot commonly known in his parish as "daft Jock," and after killing a friend for three pounds and a watch, made no effort to conceal his crime and scarcely attempted to flee. His understanding was so feeble that he believed the watch was a living creature, and when it stopped from lack of winding, he thought it had died of cold. When apprehended and questioned, he barely seemed to appreciate the difference between killing a human being and killing an ox, though his vague awareness that both of these acts were somehow wrong proved to be his undoing. He was tried, convicted, and executed.

It appears that much stress was laid on Barclay's *knowing* right from wrong, as affording indisputable proof of his being a moral agent. The reader is left to judge for himself how extensive and accurate must have been the notions on

40

on stupor. Her depression made her inefficient, and she was dismissed from a sequence of posts. She once attempted suicide because, she said, "she was ennuied at changing her place of service so often." She found another job, and two months after the suicide attempt she persuaded a shopkeeper to let her take the woman's nineteen-month-old daughter out for a walk. Instead, Cornier took the child back to her room, laid it on the bed, and severed its head with a kitchen knife. When the distraught mother came in search of her daughter two hours later, Cornier answered the door with the words, "Your child is dead," then ran to her room, hurled the head from the window, and sat down beside the corpse, bloody knife in hand, to await the arrival of the police. She readily admitted having planned the crime, and answered most questions with the simple statement, "I intended to kill the child." She could supply no motive except that the notion had possessed her mind and she felt herself destined to do it. She was aware that it was wrong, and she knew and desired the penalty.

Here was a case where the defendant clearly knew right from wrong, and yet who equally clearly, if the facts of the case were as told, should not be considered responsible. One might or might not have an emotional desire to wreak vengeance upon the perpetrator of so hideous a deed, but no one could reasonably claim that the mere awareness of having done wrong gave Henriette Cornier that malevolently purposeful consciousness, that evil intent, which the law is supposed to punish. Insanity was evidently behind the act, not viciousness, but insanity of an insidious and elusive though not uncommon type which a properly applied McNaughton test could never discern, since to the questions of policemen, lawyers, and judges the defendant would simply reply: "I did it," "I meant to do it," "I planned to do it," "I knew that it was wrong," "I know the punishment," "I expect to be punished." Beneath this seemingly competent acknowledgment of guilt would lie an emotional perversion—an illness sufficiently acute to convince anyone who finally was enabled to see it—but whose subtle indications were readily perceptible only to psychiatrists familiar with the disease through years of clinical practice.

> Insanity is a disease, and, as is the case with all other diseases, the fact of its existence is never established by a single diagnostic symptom, but by the whole body of symptoms, no particular one of which is present in every case. To distinguish the manifestations of health from those of disease requires the exercise of learning and judgment; and, if no one doubts this proposition when stated in reference to the bowels, the lungs, the heart, the liver, the kidneys, &c., what sufficient or even plausible reason is there why it should be doubted when predicated of the brain?[5]

Ray's own recommended solution to the problem of legal insanity was to replace all existing tests with some equivalent of the French Penal Code's very simple and general statement that "there is no crime nor offence when the accused was in a state of madness at the time of the action." To avoid the peculiarly unscientific courtroom procedure that consisted of having expert witnesses for each side parade their biased viewpoints, and then asking twelve jurors "taken promiscuously from the common walks of life"[6] to evaluate a complex professional controversy, Ray also suggested adopting the French system of court-appointed *experts*. Medical witnesses would be selected for their learning and competence alone, and partial immunity to the rigors of adversarial cross-examination would permit them to explain their opinions fully and objectively.

Justice Doe of New Hampshire was one jurist who was greatly influenced by Isaac Ray's work, and he had it in mind in 1866 when he filed a dissenting opinion in *Boardman* v. *Woodman*,[7] a case on testamentary capacity. The majority decision held that, as first enunciated by Lord Erskine in

Hadfield's case, *delusion* was a proper test of insanity. Justice Doe felt that it was impertinent for the law to presume to know what the test of insanity might be, particularly when the test they finally settled upon was considered wholly inadequate by the profession best qualified to know.

> If it is necessary that the law should entertain a single medical opinion concerning a single disease, it is not necessary that that opinion should be a cast-off theory of physicians of a former generation. That cannot be a fact in law, which is not a fact in science; that cannot be health in law, which is disease in fact. And it is unfortunate that courts should maintain a contest with science and the laws of nature, upon a question of fact which is within the province of science and outside the domain of our law.[8]

The law did not dare to define smallpox, fever, or any other physical ailment, and there was no apparent reason why the law should feel more at home among the immeasurably greater complexity of mental disease. The courtroom should be a place where experts presented the fruits of their knowledge, and where the relationship of that knowledge to the case at hand would be determined by the ultimate trier of fact, the jury, without the interference of arbitrary and irrelevant rules.

A mutual friend put Justice Doe in touch with Isaac Ray, and the two men began a correspondence that would result, a few years later, in the establishment of a novel form of legislation. Ray read Doe's dissenting opinion, and naturally agreed that the existing tests of civil and criminal lunacy were wrong. Nonetheless if, as Doe had written, insanity was a fact to be determined by random lay jurors, and if, as Ray gathered to be so, the law intended to excuse only those who suffered from certain kinds or degrees of insanity, and not all persons whose minds were tinged with mental disease, he saw certain practical difficulties in following his own advice and completely dispensing with tests.

Justice Doe replied that he did not really think that the law had ever wanted to restrict the insanity defense to particular forms of mental disease. The common law attitude, in his view, was simply that insanity was a disease, and that neither crimes nor valid contracts could be the product or offspring of mental disease. The causal relationship was the important aspect: whether a human agent or a pathological condition was the motivating factor behind the act. If, historically, the law seemed to have restricted the insanity defense to certain kinds or degrees of insanity, it was only because the various tests were unfortunate attempts to express this causational requirement.

With this point agreed upon, Doe and Ray readily arrived at what they believed to be the most general, simple, and just way of presenting the issue of insanity, and Doe set about having it adopted as law in New Hampshire. Doe shrewdly realized that he dare not present it as based upon Ray's opinions—which he personally acknowledged it was—lest it be promptly dismissed by jurists as a "doctor's notion,"[9] and to propose it as wholly new, from whatever source, would automatically doom it to failure. The legal profession, he explained to Ray,

> is to be convinced only by the argument that our rule is the ancient, original theory of the common law,—older than Hale or Coke. State a legal proposition as new, and you waste your time arguing in support of it. In your profession it is not so, and it is not easy for a man of science, acknowledging and struggling for progress, to understand that the only common law progress which a lawyer will admit is the progress of reviving and restoring the primeval ideas and spirit and meaning of that law.[10]

Doe did, indeed, persuade his fellow justices that his view was correct. A test case arose in 1869,[11] when Josiah Pike killed Thomas Brown with an ax, confessed to the crime, was charged with first-degree murder, and raised a defense of insanity based on claims that he suffered from dipsomania. The charge to the jury came precisely from Doe and Ray's views:

> [T]he verdict should be "not guilty by reason of insanity" if the killing was the offspring or product of mental disease in the defendant; that neither delusion nor knowledge of right and wrong, nor design or cunning in planning and executing the killing and escaping or avoiding detection, nor ability to recognize acquaintances, or to labor or transact business or manage affairs, is, as a matter of law, a test of mental disease; but that all symptoms and all tests of mental disease are purely matters of fact to be determined by the jury.[12]

Doe's concurring opinion in the case presented the same arguments as his letters to Isaac Ray, and further pointed out that the new formulation relieved the bench of its former need for hypocrisy. It was a lamentable sight to see a medical witness tell the jury that knowledge is not the *medical* test of insanity, then the judge instruct that knowledge is the *legal* test, and then finally for the judge, "forced by an impulse of humanity, as he often is, to substantially advise the jury to acquit the accused on the testimony of the experts, in violation of the test asserted by himself."[13]

Two years after *State* v. *Pike*,° this reworking of the insanity defense was affirmed in *State* v. *Jones*,[14] and the rule that the test of criminal responsibility was whether or not the act "was the offspring or product of mental disease in the defendant," also known as the New Hampshire Rule, has remained law in that state ever since.† In 1869, Isaac Ray optimistically pre-

---

° The change in rule did not help Josiah Pike himself, who was hanged on November 9, 1869.

† Oddly enough, it is impossible to say with any confidence how the New Hampshire Rule has worked out in practice in that state. Writing in 1955, the legal scholar Henry Weihofen[15] found that there had not been enough insanity defenses raised in New Hampshire since 1871 for a valid study.

dicted that *Pike* and *Jones* marked the end of the right-wrong rule. He wrote to Justice Doe, "I suppose it will finally be accepted everywhere, because I am sure it indicates the true spirit and genius of our people."[16] In this he was wrong. It was not until 1954, when Judge David Bazelon handed down the *Durham* decision in the District of Columbia Circuit Court, that anyone else followed suit. The modern problems arising from a New Hampshire non-test of insanity will be seen in the discussion of *Durham* below.

If other jurisdictions were unwilling to follow New Hampshire's sweeping abolition of all insanity tests, there was a persistent feeling, even among many who thought McNaughton correct as far as it went, that McNaughton did not go far enough. If it was legally and socially correct to acquit someone who did not know that his act was wrong, should one not also acquit a person who was unable to prevent himself from committing an act despite knowledge of its wrongfulness? If a man were compelled to commit a crime at gunpoint, or if someone stronger seized his hand and forcibly guided it through an illegal deed, no one would hold him responsible. Physicians proclaimed that mental disease, too, could threaten a man, seize control of his hand, and force him to do things against his will.

Dr. Henry Maudsley spoke of "morbid impulse" taking "despotic possession of the patient" and driving him to desperate acts in spite of himself.[17] Dr. Forbes Winslow mentioned "cases of insanity where the patient is driven, by an irresistible impulse, to destroy, after struggling, for some time, against the morbid desire, being, at the same time, perfectly conscious that he is impelled to do what is wrong both in the sight of God and man."[18] Isaac Ray himself wrote that

> . . . we have an immense mass of cases related by men of unquestionable competence and veracity, where people are *irresistibly* impelled to the commission of criminal acts while

47

fully conscious of their nature and consequences; and the force of these facts must be overcome by something more than angry declamation against visionary theories and ill-judged humanity. They are not fictions invented by medical men ... for the purpose of puzzling juries and defeating the ends of justice, but plain, unvarnished facts as they occurred in nature.[19]

The New Hampshire Rule automatically permitted evidence on such cases, but in other jurisdictions it was necessary, if the judge was willing, to inform the jurors that they need not restrict their deliberations to the narrow cognitive issues raised in the McNaughton Rule. Some courts had, in fact, already given such broadly inclusive instructions. As early as Edward Oxford's trial, Lord Denman's instructions to the jury included the mention: "If some controlling disease was, in truth, the acting power within him which he could not resist, then he will not be responsible."[20] Even at Daniel McNaughton's own trial, before it was stopped, not the judge, but the prosecutor suggested that the question was "whether at the time the prisoner committed the crime he was at that time to be regarded as a responsible agent, or whether all control of himself was taken away?" In a prominent 1844 Massachusetts case, the trial of Abner Rogers, Chief Justice Shaw asked the jury to consider "whether the prisoner in committing the homicide, acted from an irresistible and uncontrollable impulse: If so, then the act was not the act of a voluntary agent, but the involuntary act of the body, without the concurrence of a mind directing it."[21]

In general, however, jurists opposed the concept of "irresistible impulse," as it came to be known. One judge frankly stated that "I cannot see how a person who rationally comprehends the nature and quality of an act, and knows that it is wrong and criminal, can act through irresistible innocent impulse."[22] England's Lord Bramwell ridiculed the concept in one case where a witness testified, to support allegations that a defendant was subject to uncontrollable fits, that the prisoner had once been unable to resist the temptation to kill a cat. Lord Bramwell "asked if he thought he would have killed the cat if a policeman had been present. The witness answered, 'No.' His Lordship then said he supposed the impulse was irresistible only in the absence of a policeman."[23] It may have been under the inspiration of this case that some jurists proposed the "policeman at the elbow" test of irresistible impulse—that only if the defendant's compulsion was so strong that he couldn't wait until the law turned the corner would his impulse be deemed truly irresistible.°

Two factors operated in the judicial opposition to irresistible impulse. There was, on the one hand, a feeling that *all* men suffer from impulses of one sort or another, such as greed, hatred, lust, and revenge, but that the laws of God and society demand that one resist these urges. That a man should succumb to perverse inclinations, far from excusing him, is precisely what makes him a criminal. If he has trouble controlling himself, then the law will assist him: as stated in one court, "The law says to men who say they are afflicted with irresistible impulses: 'If you cannot resist an impulse in any other way, we will hang a rope in front of your eyes, and perhaps that will help.' "[24] Another judge is alleged to have said he conceded that the defendant labored under an irresistible impulse at the time he committed the crime, but that unfortunately for the defendant, two could play at that game, and the court now had an irresistible impulse to punish him.

The other, far more difficult objection to irresistible impulse was that even if one accepted the theoretical proposition that some people were prevented by mental disease from controlling

---

° It is an odd coincidence that Daniel McNaughton had shot Mr. Drummond with a policeman in sight and thus, though he should not have qualified for acquittal under a strict McNaughton Rule, he was an excellent candidate for irresistible impulse.

their behavior, there was no practical way to identify them. It would be all but impossible to determine at what point an impulse became truly irresistible, according to whatever standard one might choose, and at what point it was merely unresisted. Moreover, the unfortunate use of the word "impulse" led many people to believe that the concept applied only to a very sudden and transitory condition that would have vanished into thin air by the time the defendant reached the courtroom, leaving an apparently normal individual claiming momentary past insanity.

The purely cognitive McNaughton Rule theoretically, if not always in practice, said that acquitted lunatics were very definitely different from other people: they did not know right from wrong, as do the rest of us, or they might not know exactly what it was that they had done in the first place. The standards of criminal insanity under McNaughton were more liberal than in olden times, when only the most flagrantly and notoriously insane were excused, but using the rule one should still be able to demonstrate to the satisfaction of twelve strangers that the defendant was distinctively odd. One could bring out objective evidence proving that he did not know he had done wrong: he neglected to take rudimentary precautions or did not flee, or his chain of reasoning led clear out of the realm of logic.

The volitional "irresistible impulse" test allowed the bounds of legal insanity to creep uncomfortably close to normal life and its daily evils. Almost anyone could claim lack of control, and if the defendant came into court conceding knowledge of his wrongdoing and admitting the purpose and logic of his acts, there was little objective evidence to support or disprove his claims that he couldn't help himself—could not help himself so much, in fact, that we should feel sympathy rather than outrage. The jurors, it seemed, might be left entirely at the mercy of two sets of psychiatrists testifying that yes, he could, or no, he couldn't, resist, and basing their opinions on an arcane branch of learning inaccessible to the general public.

By the beginning of the twentieth century, about half of the American states had adopted irresistible impulse as a supplement to the McNaughton Rule. England and some other states specifically rejected it, while the rest left the matter vague. A fairly common sentiment was that there was sufficient flexibility inherent in the trial process that a person so truly deranged that his impulses were irresistible would somehow not be convicted, whatever the letter of the law. It was better to make benevolent use of a strict law than to alter the law itself.

5

OPPOSITION TO THE
INSANITY DEFENSE

During the better part of a century there were few further changes in the tests of criminal responsibility, despite the fact that the scientific view of behavior underwent radical transformations. The two views of humanity, the legal and the scientific, simply did not share enough common ground for a continuing useful dialogue. Psychiatrists claimed that mental defects stemmed from hereditary, organic, and chemical disorders; many criminologists, after Lombroso, maintained that there was a physically determined "criminal type"; psychoanalysis interpreted much of conscious behavior in terms of unconscious forces dating from early, forgotten childhood events; and behaviorists viewed the thinking person in each of us as a sort of automaton whose apparent consciousness was merely the epiphenomenon of a constellation of stimuli and responses. However reasonable these theories might be in some ultimate, explanatory sense, they were useless in the daily world, where each person knew, from personal experience, that he was free to choose his own course of action, and where the law had to assume that such things existed as an evil will and blameworthiness. As late as 1965, one American judge, when faced with a psychoanalytic interpretation of a murder, felt obligated to say, "Now this is interesting, and I will not quarrel with any of it. But the question is whether it has anything to do with the crime of murder. I think it does not."[1] In the far distant future, when everything is explained to the last decimal point of precision, free will and personal responsibility may prove to be fictions, but in the meantime they are very useful fictions that help society to function sanely.

Far from Isaac Ray's fond hope that the New Hampshire Rule expressed the will of the people and would quickly spread everywhere, the more the matter was discussed the more people felt that even McNaughton was too liberal and that the insanity defense itself was a sham. Psychiatry made progress in diagnosing and classifying mental disorders, but it was an odd and mistrusted profession. Other branches of science could demonstrate their worth in irrefutably tangible form. Other physicians could relieve pain and cure disease. The psychiatrist, however, whose ability to cure acute cases was small, and whose successes elsewhere were often indistinguishable from natural remission, claimed expertise in an area that the merest layman thought he understood: other people. Moreover, laymen felt that their own perception was more practical and less gullible than that of psychiatrists, who were frequently depicted in popular fiction as being readily duped by families with ulterior motives into committing perfectly sane relatives, and otherwise prompt to put a pathological interpretation on nearly any bit of behavior, particularly the criminal.

Mark Twain wrote an article in 1870[2] describing, among others, the case of an Ohio man named Baldwin, who was tried on a charge of murder. Proof of the deed was ironclad, but according to Twain, it was demonstrated, at great expense to Baldwin's wealthy family, that the defendant had gone insane on the morning of the crime and not recovered himself until a few hours after the victim was dead. "This same Baldwin had momentary fits of insanity twice afterward, and on both occasions killed people he had grudges against." Such unhappy coincidences seemed to be more and more frequent. "Insanity certainly is on the increase in the world, and crime is dying out," Twain complained.

> Is not this insanity plea becoming rather common? Is it not so common that the reader confidently expects to see it offered in every criminal case that comes before the courts? And is it not so cheap, and so common, and often so trivial, that the reader smiles in derision when the newspaper mentions it? And is it not curious to note how very often it wins acquittal for the prisoner? Of late years it does not seem possible for a man to so conduct himself, before killing another man, as not to be manifestly insane. If he talks about the stars, he is insane. If he appears nervous and uneasy an hour before the killing, he is insane. If he weeps over a great grief, his friends shake their heads, and fear that he is "not right." If, an hour after the murder, he seems ill at ease, preoccupied and excited, he is unquestionably insane.
>
> Really what we want now, is not laws against crime, but a law against *insanity*. There is where the true evil lies.

Twain was hardly alone in these sentiments. In 1871, no less a person than Congressman James A. Garfield is supposed to have written to a judge congratulating him upon his rejection of an insanity defense. "The whole country owes you a debt of gratitude for brushing away the wicked absurdity which has lately been palmed off on the country as law in the subject of insanity. If the thing had gone much further all that a man would need to secure immunity from murder would be to tear his hair and rave a little, and then kill his man."[3] A decade later President Garfield himself was assassinated by Charles Julius Guiteau, who is retrospectively regarded as having been quite insane and who raised the defense at his trial. At the time, however, though few people denied Guiteau's marked eccentricities, it seemed fairly obvious to everyone that, under the circumstances, given the identity of the victim, the killer must surely be convicted, condemned, and hanged, as he was.

With such strong feelings against the insanity defense, it was only natural that several attempts should be made to abolish it, particularly since, with the gradual decline in capital punishment and the rise of penitentiaries and asylums, the fates of convicts and lunatics were growing more similar anyway. The first attempt, perhaps, was that of Sir V. Blake before the House of Lords in 1843, following Daniel Mc-Naughton's acquittal. He suggested that the insanity defense be abolished "in cases of murder, or attempts to murder, except where it can be proved that the person accused was publicly known and reputed to be a maniac, and not afflicted by partial insanity only."[4] Though the Lords were deeply concerned about abuses of the insanity defense, this measure evidently seemed much too drastic, and no one seconded the motion.

A slightly more serious and rather peculiar attempt at abolition, again in England and once more under Queen Victoria, took place nearly forty years later. In 1882 an unemployed grocery clerk named Roderick Maclean shot at the Queen in the Windsor railway station, and was captured by Eton boys, who beat him over the head with their umbrellas. At trial, nearly everyone conceded that the presumption of sanity was fairly met and overcome: Maclean's brain had been damaged by a head wound as a child, he had been diagnosed insane eight years earlier by Henry Maudsley, one of the most distinguished specialists in the land, he was epileptic, and he had spent a year in a lunatic asylum. He had delusions of persecution and believed, among other things, that the entire English people conspired against him and wore blue as a symbol of their determined enmity; "if they do not cease wearing blue I will commit murder," he wrote to his sister shortly before the crime.

Even the press, which had initially hoped for Maclean's

conviction, ultimately applauded the justness of his acquittal by reason of insanity—in part, it appears, because the verdict seemed to prove that none but a lunatic would try to kill the English Queen. "It is a remarkable fact—" the London *Times* editors wrote,[5] "perhaps unique in history—that never in her long reign has [Queen Victoria] had reason to fear violence which could be in the remotest way connected with politics. The potboy, Edward Oxford, who would fain have posed as a political conspirator, proved in the end to be a mad potboy and nothing more." All assassination attempts against Victoria, of which there had been some half dozen, stemmed not from sane political motives, as was true in Europe and the United States, but from "wounded vanity, disappointed ambition, craze for notoriety, and the combination of ill-regulated aspirations for distinction with defective faculties."

The fact that English political assassins were individual lunatics rather than reasoning conspirators may have reassured the editors of the *Times*, but it did little to satisfy an outraged Queen Victoria, who owed her life to poor marksmanship rather than to deluded motives. "Insane he may have been," she said of Roderick Maclean, "but not guilty he most certainly was not." When assured that this was the verdict prescribed by law, it is said that she replied, "If that is the law, then the law must be changed," and changed the law was. At her insistence, Prime Minister Gladstone asked the Lord Chief Justice and Attorney General what alterations might be made. Gladstone himself thought there was no need, realizing that a verdict of not guilty by reason of insanity was, in practical terms, a life sentence,[6] but he also supposed that its unfortunate use of the words "not guilty" might produce "dangerous misapprehensions in morbid minds,"[7] and lead criminally inclined lunatics to believe themselves immune to the law.

As a result of Maclean's trial, Parliament passed the Trial of Lunatics Act of 1883, which abolished the verdict of not guilty by reason of insanity in England, and stipulated that in such cases "the jury shall return a special verdict to the effect that the accused was guilty of the act or omission charged against him, but was insane . . . at the time when he did the act or made the omission."[8] The act did not stipulate that anything different be *done* with those people found "guilty but insane." They were still committed to Broadmoor at Her Majesty's Pleasure, which usually lasted until they died. The practical effect of the Trial of Lunatics Act, then, was quite invisible, and many legal scholars attacked such hollow legislation as superfluous and silly. "Why the present statute was passed it is difficult to understand," wrote the editor of the *Practical Statutes of the Session 1883*,[9] "unless it be ascribed to that officiousness which will not leave well enough alone."

If the disposition of those who met the McNaughton criteria was unchanged, for several decades afterward there was, nonetheless, a nagging doubt among English jurists as to whether or not the 1883 act had, as Victoria evidently desired, transformed the technical predicament of these offenders from acquitted lunatics to convicted lunatics. The issue was not decided until 1914, when the case of *Felstead* v. *Rex* was appealed to the House of Lords.[10] Felstead had been tried for wounding his wife with intent to do grievous bodily harm, and was found guilty but insane. He appealed this verdict, saying that he was quite willing to serve out a fixed term in prison, but did not care to be held at His Majesty's Pleasure in a criminal lunatic asylum. The House of Lords decided, however, that "if he was insane at the time of committing the act he could not have had a mens rea, and his state of mind could not have been that which is involved in the use of the term 'feloniously' or 'maliciously.' "[11] Consequently, whatever may have been the intent of the 1883 legislature when passing the Trial of Lunatics Act, a verdict of guilty but insane meant only that "upon the facts proved, the jury would have found him guilty of the offense had it not been established to their satisfaction that he was at the time not responsible for his actions." As one commentator paraphrased it, "guilty but insane" thus might be construed as finding "that prisoner had a guilty mind but was out of it at the time," or that he was "guilty, but not guilty."[12]

Unfortunately for Mr. Felstead, this decision meant that he had been acquitted, and since an acquittal could not be appealed, he had to stay right where he was. This legal stance was confirmed slightly later in *In re Houghton*:[13] a man found guilty but insane of murdering his father and brother was permitted to inherit the spoils of his crime because the apparent conviction was in fact an acquittal, hence there was no crime, there were no spoils, and he was naturally entitled to the estate of his relatives after their untimely demise.

The next attempt to abolish the insanity defense took place in the United States, and was at least partly spurred by public indignation over the acquittal of Harry K. Thaw. Thaw was a Pittsburgh millionaire who, on June 25, 1906, shot and killed the renowned architect and socialite Stanford White during a concert at New York City's old Madison Square Garden. White had once been involved with Thaw's wife, Evelyn Nesbit, and Thaw had conceived a monumental hatred for White not only as his wife's former lover, but, as he saw him, as a symbol of all depraved men who ravish women and seduce the innocent.

Thaw pleaded not guilty, and the defense tried to portray Stanford White in such an unfavorable light that Thaw's shooting of him would appear a morally justifiable act. The defense vacillated between trying to use and to avoid an insanity defense, and perhaps hoped that, if the jury would not choose to acquit outright, it would at least make sympathetic use of the insanity verdict to express its covert approval of the defendant's act. "[I]f Thaw is insane," argued defense counsel at one point,

it is with a species of insanity known from the Canadian

border to the Gulf. If you expert gentlemen ask me to give
it a name, I suggest that you label it *Dementia Americana.*
It is that species of insanity that inspires of every American
to believe his home is sacred. It is that species of insanity
that persuades an American that whoever violates the sanctity
of his home or the purity of his wife or daughter has forfeited
the protection of the laws of this state or any other state.[14]

The jury deliberated for several days, and returned to
announce that they were hopelessly deadlocked: seven in favor
of a first-degree murder conviction, five for an acquittal by
reason of insanity. At a second trial, in 1908, Thaw was
acquitted by reason of insanity and ordered sent to New York's
Matteawan asylum for the criminally insane.

Thaw's family, lawyers, and money had so successfully
portrayed Stanford White as a villain and Harry K. Thaw as a
wronged husband that the acquittal was initially widely applauded, but in the face of Thaw's subsequent behavior popular
sympathy evaporated, then turned against him. Thaw drove to
Grand Central Station in his own automobile, and held a party
in a private railroad car on the way to Matteawan. At Fishkill,
he treated his friends to a champagne dinner, and it was only
at midnight that a deputy sheriff persuaded him to check in at
the hospital. Though Matteawan was a locked state asylum,
Thaw was given a suite and permitted to go out for dinner
and drives in the countryside; several doctors who would not
respect these privileges were relieved of their duties. Backed
by the family wealth, Thaw soon began an endless sequence
of legal petitions. Four months after his trial, he asked to be
released. When this was refused, he requested transfer to a
private sanatorium, and when the court refused that, he asked
for a jury trial to determine his sanity. He appealed the denial
of this petition up through all the New York courts and finally
to the U.S. Supreme Court. When that didn't work, he started
all over again with another series of writs.

The legal fraternity was infuriated by this grotesque spectacle, and in 1909 a special New York State Bar Association committee recommended that the law be changed. Without naming names, the committee cited as an example of the insanity defense's abuse the case of "[a] youthful debauchee, of great wealth, trained to believe that his money gave him a right of freedom from all restraints, whether imposed by law or the rules of decency, inheriting an abnormality of mind likely to develop into homicidal acts, leading a debased and ignoble life, without a thought of the responsibilities which wealth imposes upon its owner, [who] commits a foul and cowardly murder in a public resort."[15] The committee felt certain this debauchee would eventually gain his release, since he possessed zealous counsel, unscrupulous experts, and a bottomless purse, and the law permitted him to file writs of habeas corpus for as long as it took to find one judge "whose head is not able to control his heart."

To remedy the situation, the New York State Bar Association committee recommended, on the one hand, severely limiting an insanity acquittee's right to file writs and, on the other hand, to abolish the anachronistic insanity acquittal altogether. "Has not the time come in the development of our system of penology to relegate to the realm of the obsolete, the assumption that an insane man cannot commit crime? In other words, ought we not to abolish the defense of insanity, and leave as the one issue to the petit jury, did the accused do the forbidden deed? If he did not, he is innocent; if he did, he is guilty, and with the state of his mind at that time the jury has nothing to do. . . . [H]owever legally right under existing legal concepts, it is really wrong, sociologically wrong, to find a man not guilty on the ground of insanity."[16]

Harry K. Thaw, too, was disenchanted with the existing legal system. In March 1913 he lost patience, walked out the front gates of Matteawan, climbed into a waiting car, and drove to Canada. It was almost two years before he returned to New York, and seven months later a court declared him sane.°

Nothing came of the New York State Bar Association's recommendations, but in the same year, probably impelled by the same case, the state of Washington did abolish its insanity defense. Under their new law:

> It shall be no defense to a person charged with the commission of a crime, that at the time of its commission, he was unable by reason of his insanity, idiocy, or imbecility, to comprehend the nature and quality of the act committed, or to understand that it was wrong; or that he was afflicted with a morbid propensity to commit prohibited acts; nor shall any testimony or other proof thereof be admitted in evidence.[17]

The defendant could no longer be acquitted by reason of insanity, but if, following conviction, the court determined that he satisfied the McNaughton criteria it could, at its discretion, order him committed to a state hospital.[18] It is not clear what the legislature wished to have happen to mentally ill convicts who later recovered. The New York committee recommended that they remain hospitalized unless pardoned,[19] though a possible alternative would be a transfer to prison.

Washington's abolition of the insanity defense was successfully challenged one year after its passage. In October 1909, Martin Strasburg was convicted of assault in the first degree for shooting and wounding a man; a defense of insanity was barred by the new law. Strasburg appealed to the state supreme court on grounds that he had been denied his consti-

---

° In January 1917 Thaw was arrested and charged with kidnapping. According to the indictment, the previous Christmas Eve he had picked up a young man in a Kansas City ice cream parlor, taken him to a hotel room, and beaten him unconscious with a whip. To avoid a trial, Thaw's family brought him back to Pennsylvania, took out a commission in lunacy, and had him committed to the privately run Pennsylvania Hospital in Philadelphia. He remained there until 1924, and was never tried on the charges.

tutional guarantee not to be deprived of life, liberty, or property without due process of law. By "due process" the appellant meant procedures in accordance with the general rules of jurisprudence, which among other things gave a defendant the right to contest elements of the charge against him, including the mental component of the crime. By eliminating psychiatric testimony, the state had rendered him unable to cast reasonable doubt upon his capacity to form the requisite felonious intent.

The state, in contesting Strasburg's appeal, maintained that the legislature had the authority to remove the intent element from any crime and to make it a strict liability offense. As examples it mentioned laws against the sale of adulterated food, selling alcoholic beverages to minors, Indians, drunks, or insane people, living off the earnings of a prostitute, adultery, incest, statutory rape, and involuntary manslaughter. None of them had an intent requirement: eliminating these offenses was seen to be so much in the interest of the general public welfare that the police power of the state was entitled to punish even those who were not conscious of having done wrong. In 1910 a butcher was convicted of selling unsound meat even though no test he could reasonably have been expected to perform would have detected its unsoundness.[20]

Intentless "public welfare offenses," however, usually involve charges that, though criminal, are closer to civil negligence cases in their nature, consequences, and the social stigma that attaches to the offender. The penalties are generally relatively small fines rather than imprisonment, and the particular crimes are often ones in which it would be extremely difficult to demonstrate intent even when there *had* been wanton neglect. It is an entirely different matter to abolish the intent elements from a major felony offense and say that the mere commission of the act carries proof that one had competently and malevolently chosen to do it. The Washington Supreme Court was unwilling to do this. Moreover, it seemed as patently evident to them as it would to the House of Lords in *Felstead* that consideration of the legal question of intent could not be limited to the external circumstances surrounding the commission of the act, but must take into account, in one way or another, the internal workings of the defendant's mind. Holding that the due process clause of the state and federal constitutions guaranteed a defendant the right to a trial by jury "upon all questions of fact, and this includes the substantive fact of the sanity of the accused at the time of the act charged,"[21] the court determined that the legislature had exceeded its constitutional power, and voided the new law.

A similar attempt at abolition was made two decades later by the state of Mississippi, which in its Laws of 1928[22] mandated that insanity should be no defense, though mental state might be taken into consideration during the sentencing phase of the trial. The law was similarly knocked down in the first case that came up, that of Frank Sinclair, who was accused of murder. Sinclair was found guilty, but insane, and in light of his mental illness, rather than hanging he was given a life sentence, which he appealed on constitutional grounds. The Supreme Court of Mississippi remarked in its decision that

> [I]n the light of legal history in all of the civilized nations of the world it is almost impossible to believe that a legislature at this advanced age would pass a law to the effect that insanity shall no longer be a defense to the charge of crime. How this act passed both the Houses of the legislature and was approved by the governor of the state, who was so prone to veto acts of the present legislature on constitutional grounds, is a mystery to the legal fraternity of Mississippi.[23]

According to the court, the statute conflicted not only with the due process clauses of the U.S. and Mississippi constitutions, just as the Washington court had maintained, but also violated state and federal constitutional protections against cruel and unusual punishment. To convict a man of murder when he

63

had no inkling of having done wrong was most decidedly cruel and unusual. In a concurring opinion, Justice Griffith said that an insane person, who "is no more than a frame of bones and muscles," utterly bereft of reason, is no more responsible for committing a criminal offense "than would a dead body found naked on the street be indictable for an indecent exposure."[24] He estimated that for every false use of the insanity defense there were twenty-five defendants who eluded justice through a sham plea of self-defense, yet no one dreamed of abolishing self-defense. It seemed odd and erroneous to suppose that insanity was in any way a less fundamental issue.

The insanity defense, which once relied on the sufferance and whim of monarchs, was now so firmly wed to the basic tenets of law that all the power of a legislature could no longer eradicate it. Even attempts to limit the defense or its abuse sometimes only seemed to make matters worse, as was the case with California's long experiment with a bifurcated trial system.

In 1925, disturbed by the rising postwar crime rate, the California legislature created a Commission for the Reform of Criminal Procedure intended to "provide this state with the most efficient system for the swift and certain administration of criminal justice."[25] As the wording suggests, this meant making things easier for the prosecution,[26] and the commission examined a wide range of problem areas, including the insanity defense.

California's insanity defense at the time was already fairly rigid: irresistible impulse was not allowed, and the courts applied the McNaughton Rule according to narrow, strictly cognitive interpretations. It is unlikely that things were worse than anywhere else, but the commission thought that was quite bad enough. There were several difficulties with the defense, but the one that disturbed the commissioners most was the fact that defendants pleading insanity were permitted to introduce vast quantities of personal background information into the trial. Whereas in a normal criminal proceeding narrow limits are set on the range of evidence that is admissible as relevant to the case, in an insanity trial this range is considerably broader, since all sorts of facts and incidents not directly related to the specific offense might nonetheless help to illustrate the nature of the defendant's mind and, by inference, to establish his insanity at the time of the crime. The commissioners believed, however, that defendants with no sincere hope of succeeding in an insanity defense often raised one anyway in order to gain the opportunity to haul in a sob story, play on the sympathies of the jury, and otherwise confuse a very simple question of guilt or innocence.[27]

The commission's proposed solution, which the legislature readily adopted,[28] was to split insanity trials in two. A defendant claiming lack of criminal responsibility due to mental disease or defect would enter a dual plea of "not guilty" and "not guilty by reason of insanity." At his first trial, he would be conclusively presumed to be sane, and the sole question for the jury would be, Is he guilty or not guilty? The jury could not be swayed in its verdict by stories about the prisoner's unfortunate childhood, wretched home life, or years in and out of insane asylums, because no psychiatric testimony or other evidence on the defendant's personal misery and emotional idiosyncrasies would be allowed. If, at the end of the trial, the defendant was acquitted, his acquittal would be absolute, and he would go free, whether crazy or not. If he was convicted but had also pleaded insanity, he would move on to a second trial, before the same jury, at which the only issue would be his mental state. If found sane, he would go to prison. If found insane, the earlier conviction would be negated and the court would commit him to a mental hospital. The defendant might, if he chose, also plead "not guilty by reason of insanity" alone, signifying a guilty plea on the facts but a plea of not guilty due to lack of responsibility.

This bifurcated trial procedure° not only clarified the issues, but promised to avoid some of the more inane circumstances one occasionally encountered, as when a defendant wishing to contest both the facts and his sanity was obliged to tell an understandably incredulous jury that either he didn't do it and was sane, or he had done it but was crazy at the time. There were other problems, however, which the California legislature had not anticipated, and they concerned, once again, the question of intent.

Felstead v. *Rex* in England and *Strasburg* v. *State* in America had firmly stated a policy that mental illness could not be completely divorced from the issue of criminal responsibility because guilt and legal insanity could not coexist. The situation was less clear, however, in cases where there was mental illness that did not meet the threshold of legal insanity. Could a defendant, for example, be too crazy to commit first-degree murder, but sane enough to commit voluntary manslaughter? Could evidence of mental disease or abnormal mental state reduce the degree of a crime rather than negate it altogether?

In some circumstances the answer was that it definitely could. Intoxication, for example, was generally viewed as an aggravating rather than a mitigating circumstance, but a number of state and Supreme Court decisions had held that in certain situations intoxication could interfere with the formation of intent. In *Hopt* v. *People*,[29] decided in 1881, the U.S. Supreme Court stated that "[w]hen a statute establishing different degrees of murder requires deliberate premeditation in order to constitute murder in the first degree, the question whether the accused is in such a condition of mind, by reason of

° California was not the first state to experiment with a bifurcated trial. In 1878 Wisconsin had instituted a curiously reversed dual procedure, in which the defendant was first tried on the question of insanity, and subsequently tried on the facts. The jury was thus placed in the odd position of having to decide legal insanity with respect to the facts of the case before having ascertained what those facts were. The Wisconsin statute was sustained on appeal, but was repealed by the legislature in 1911.

66

drunkenness or otherwise, as to be capable of deliberate premeditation, necessarily becomes a material subject of consideration by the jury."°

In addition, even a relatively uncontroversial mitigating circumstance such as "provocation" was legally defined in terms of the impairment of intent by an abnormal mental state, so that a man whose passions had overcome and submerged his reason might be held less responsible than if he had methodically plotted his deed. Courts in at least eight states, moreover,[31] had more or less explicitly stated that mental disease or defect short of full legal insanity could negate intent elements of a crime. In California itself a judge in 1914 had instructed a jury:

> [W]here the accused is charged with deliberate homicide and offers evidence to show that the condition of his mind through predisposition [to insanity] was such that he was incapable of deliberation, the reasonable doubt as to such capacity for deliberation should be resolved in favor of the accused to the extent that it acquits him of the higher grade and convicts him of the lower grade of the offense.[32]

A few other states had specifically rejected the concept that mental illness could reduce a charge, though in most it was left vague. Courts were understandably reluctant to encourage the insidious spread of an unpopular defense, and from a practical point of view it seemed difficult enough for a jury to decide whether a defendant was sane or insane, without imposing upon it the further burden of subdividing insanity into subtle degrees of severity. In these states, however, there was no bifurcation of the trial, and the exclusion of psychiatric

---

° This could sometimes lead to absurd results. In one case,[30] a man formed a deliberate and premeditated design to kill someone, then went out and got drunk to nerve himself for the deed. The court ruled that he had been so intoxicated at the time of the killing that he was unable to premeditate, and could consequently not be convicted of first-degree murder.

testimony on intent did not seem so harsh, since it was admissible on the issue of insanity, and the jurors deliberated everything at once.

For more than two decades, California courts supported the legislature's decision. The first two attacks on the bifurcated trial,[33] both decided on the same day of 1928, adequately sum up both the objections to the new law and the courts' reply. Both defendants were charged with first-degree murder, both pleaded "not guilty" and "not guilty by reason of insanity," and both were convicted. Appeals in both cases contended that the defendants had been denied due process and their right to a jury trial because the court had forbidden introduction of evidence for consideration by the jury during the guilt phase, showing that due to abnormal mental conditions they had been unable to form intent elements required for a first-degree murder conviction. One also claimed that the two-trial system placed him in double jeopardy.

The court perfunctorily rejected these arguments. "Due process" meant no more than "law in the regular course of administration, according to prescribed forms and in accordance with the general rules for the protection of individual rights,"[34] and since, as the court claimed, the new legislation involved only procedural changes, the defendant's substantive rights were precisely what they had been before. The court was inclined to view the insanity defense not only as a monolithic concept that was not divisible into fine gradations, but as a "plea of confession and avoidance"[35] which either worked or did not work, whether in one trial or two, and which did not appreciably alter the material facts of the case. "The insanity of a defendant cannot be used for the purpose of reducing his crime from murder in the first degree to murder in the second degree. If responsible at all in this respect, he is responsible in the same degree as a sane man, and if he is not responsible at all he is entitled to an acquittal in both degrees."[36] As for the double jeopardy issue, the court maintained that the two segments were not separate trials, but merely separate phases of the same trial tried before the same jury, and that, far from placing the defendant in double jeopardy, the second phase gave him a chance to escape a jeopardy into which he had already placed himself.

For twenty years, matters stood there, but in 1949 the dam keeping psychiatric testimony from the guilt phase trial was broken in the case of *People* v. *Wells.*[37] Wesley Robert Wells was serving a life sentence at Folsom State Prison when he threw a cuspidor at a guard, injuring him. Under the California Penal Code at the time, a death sentence was mandatory for a prisoner serving a life sentence who committed an assault with malice aforethought. In the guilt phase of Wells's trial, the judge, following two decades of tradition, excluded expert testimony intended to show that due to mental abnormality the defendant had a particularly low "threshold of fear," reacted differently from most people to fearsome situations, and may have attacked the guard believing that he was acting in self-defense—assertions that, if accepted, would have removed the malicious nature of the assault and spared Wells's life. Wells was convicted in the guilt phase, his insanity plea did not succeed, and he was sentenced to death.

The case stood out both because the statute under which Wells was convicted seemed unjust, and because the critical determining factor was, precisely, a state of mind. Wells appealed to the state supreme court, which arrived at a curiously mixed and agile conclusion. It now seemed clear to the justices that mental evidence negating a specific intent element could not be excluded from the guilt phase of a trial. If intoxication could diminish the degree of a crime, surely mental illness might also do so. The mere fact that a defendant might eventually have a chance to prove legal insanity did not safeguard his due process right to contest specific elements of the actual charge against him.[38]

Rather than completely dismantle the bifurcated trial system, however, the justices arrived at their own subtle subdivision of mental illness, and maintained that though psychiatric testimony should be admissible during the guilt phase of the trial, it would be aimed toward a different issue than legal insanity.

> As a general rule, on the not guilty plea, evidence, otherwise competent, tending to show that the defendant, who at this stage is conclusively presumed sane, either *did* or *did not,* in committing the overt act, possess the specific essential mental state, is admissible, but evidence tending to show legal sanity or legal insanity is not admissible. Thus, if the proffered evidence tends to show not merely that he *did* or *did not,* but rather that because of legal insanity he *could* not, entertain the specific intent or other essential mental state, then that evidence is inadmissible under the not guilty plea and is admissible only on the trial on the plea of not guilty by reason of insanity.[39]

This decision did salvage the bifurcated trial, but at the expense of some damage to logic. The distinction between admissible and inadmissible evidence was hopelessly vague and somewhat absurd. Obviously a person who *could not* entertain specific intent *did not* form that intent, and in fact there could be little better proof that someone did not do something than a demonstration that he was inherently incapable of doing it. Yet the court ruled that a showing of incapacity was properly within the domain of the insanity defense and could not be presented during the guilt phase. One dissenting justice labeled this a paradoxical absurdity tantamount to saying "that blindness in one eye will absolve a person from guilt, but that two sightless eyes will constitute no defense."[40]

Dr. Bernard Diamond, who was called into the *Wells* case

when it was appealed to the U.S. Supreme Court,° does not think that the lawyers who filed the original appeal had any intention of instigating a major reform in California criminal procedure; "it was more an instance of using any device possible to save from the gas chamber a doomed defendant who had been convicted under an impossibly rigid statute."[41] Once the dam had been broken, however, there was no stopping the seepage, flow, and then flood of psychiatric testimony into the guilt phase trial.

In the 1959 case *People* v. *Gorshen*,[42] where an overt attempt was made to force major changes in California procedure, the court specifically ruled that psychiatric testimony was relevant in the guilt phase of the trial, and that mental illness short of legal insanity could negate malice, deliberation, and other subjective intent elements of a crime, and, for example, reduce the degree of homicide from murder to manslaughter. This principle was expanded five years later in *People* v. *Wolff*,[43] a homicide case against a fifteen-year-old boy who had beaten his mother to death with an ax handle so that he would have free run of her house and could lure people there for sexual purposes. He was diagnosed as chronically schizophrenic, yet an insanity plea failed, and since the circumstances of the crime and his own confession of guilt satisfied the traditional requirements of an intent to kill, malice aforethought, deliberation, and premeditation, he was convicted of first-degree murder. The appeal court, however, reduced the conviction to second-degree murder after deciding that an evaluation of the defendant's ability to premeditate and deliberate "must include consideration of the somewhat limited

° The California court's decision, though it opened the guilt trial to psychiatric testimony, did not help Wesley Wells, since the court held that in his particular case the error of excluding such testimony had been harmless. The evidence presented, the court said, including some of Wells's own testimony, conclusively proved malice. His death sentence was affirmed, the U.S. Supreme Court refused to hear the case, and his life was spared only when the governor commuted his sentence. The statute under which he had been convicted was subsequently repealed.

extent to which this defendant could *maturely and meaningfully reflect* upon the gravity of his contemplated act."[44]

Two years later this principle was expanded further still, when a judge determined that, for a defendant to have malice, he must be able to "comprehend his duty to govern his actions in accord with the duty imposed by law,"[45] which was remarkably close to the terms of an insanity defense. As one critic has commented, "Only a medieval scholastic theologian could discover any substantial difference between a defendant incapable of comprehending his duty to obey the law and a defendant incapable of understanding the wrongfulness of his act."[46] Nearly identical testimony addressing nearly identical issues was now admissible during both phases of the bifurcated trial, and a defendant could aim both at a reduction in charge due to mental illness, and at a complete negation of the charge due to insanity.

What had begun as an effort to restrict the insanity defense thus perversely made matters worse. It was rather like the enchanted broom in Goethe's "The Sorcerer's Apprentice": when split in two, each shattered piece took on a life of its own and marched on undaunted, continuing its uncontrollable work with redoubled industry. Other measures were eventually necessary to curb the unwieldy proliferation of diminished capacity and the insanity defense in California's courts. The defense of insanity, originally a unique exception to the law, was rapidly and sometimes maladroitly being woven into the tissue of the law. Identifying insanity with a lack of *mens rea* suggested that the sane and the insane criminal merely lay at different points on a continuous spectrum of legal responsibility—an implication quite far removed from the traditional view.

6

THE *DURHAM*
EXPERIMENT

There appear to be regular alternations between periods when
public concern over the insanity defense is greatest and
attempts are made to restrict it, and times when the clamor
for law and order is at a relative ebb and insanity standards
are relaxed in response to protests from the intellectual community. During the thirties and forties, very little changed in
the field; with the Depression and the Second World War
there were far more urgent social issues to consider than the
remote fringes of criminal law. But in the prosperous postwar
years there was a new drive toward understanding and aiding
sick and distressed members of society, and in the early 1950s
there was an abrupt surge of interest and faith in psychiatry
and related fields. The ranks of American psychiatrists had
been swelled by the German and East European practitioners
who fled to this country before the war, and now their students
and disciples, too, were entering professional life. The mental
casualties of World War II had brought new government and
legislative attention to the problem of psychiatric disorders,
with the result that the Veterans Administration began opening
vast psychiatric facilities, and in 1948, the federal government
established the National Institute of Mental Health.

The new decade saw the introduction of chlorpromazine

and meprobamate, the first in a family of psychoactive agents that would revolutionize the nature of institutional care and give new hope for eventual cures to the worst chronic mental disorders. Psychiatric and particularly psychoanalytic theories of human nature enjoyed a certain vogue in intellectual circles, and the general public was more receptive to medical interpretations of criminal behavior than it had ever been before. When, from 1949 to 1953, a British royal commission studied the topic of capital punishment, fully one-fourth of its final report concerned the insanity defense and the relationship between mental illness, crime, and punishment.[1]

This increased acceptance was not immediately apparent in practical terms, for psychiatrists felt that they entered a courtroom as expert witnesses at the risk of personal humiliation and perhaps some loss of professional self-esteem. "The courtroom setting, which is so familiar to lawyers, is to most physicians very uncongenial," wrote Dr. Manfred Guttmacher, one of the most prestigious forensic psychiatrists.[2]

> In many ways it is repulsive to him. He is accustomed to be listened to with respect when his opinion is sought by a colleague or by a patient. He is used to being his own boss; under our American system he takes orders from no man. In the trial situation everything is changed. . . . Instead of having his views received with the respect and deference to which he had been accustomed, he is likely on cross-examination to have them ridiculed, misstated, and twisted into absurdities. His intelligence and his professional competence will in all likelihood be questioned, and often his integrity will be impugned.

As a consequence, many psychiatrists flatly refused all forensic cases. Though the psychiatrist's subject touched the very heart of the issue of responsibility and blame, he appeared in a courtroom on the same footing as the ballistics man, the handwriting analyst, the structural engineer, or any other expert who came bearing soft "opinion" evidence. His subtle perception of human beings, the fruit of his long training, was not evaluated and disputed on scientific grounds, but was assailed through the infuriating tricks of the trial lawyer.

A psychiatrist might be asked whether he had often testified at insanity trials before. If he said no, opposing counsel deftly implied that, then, he could not possibly know what he was talking about. If the answer was yes, he could usually be made to admit that he generally appeared for one side—that for which he was appearing right now—thus suggesting that he was a hired gun or a "psychiatric whore," an impression heavily stressed when opposing counsel knowingly inquired how much he had been paid to testify today that, as the case may be, the defendant was or was not legally insane. The psychiatrist was invariably asked how long after the crime he had examined the defendant, and since it was always at least a matter of days, and frequently of weeks or months, an attorney could raise his eyebrows and marvel that from such a distant vantage point the doctor could diagnose the defendant's mental state all the way back at the precise time when the crime took place.

A psychiatrist whose role was only to make a medical evaluation could not and needed not know all the details of the crime, and consequently one favorite prosecutorial gimmick was to dredge up some detail the prosecutor felt reasonably sure the defense psychiatrist would not know, and to ask if he knew it. The psychiatrist would admit he did not. "Well, doctor, *had* you known, would it have changed your opinion?" If the witness said no, his opinion might seem impossibly rigid, formed without regard for the facts. If he said yes, he looked the fool.

In his testimony, too, the psychiatric witness might be baffled and exasperated by the opposing side. He could be asked loaded questions, or instructed to diagnose a hypothetical case which was identical to the one at hand in all but a few critical aspects. Since psychiatry is as much an art as a science, its complex conclusions must often be expressed through intricate verbal imagery, yet the witness might be told to answer yes or no, or cut short after a partial response. He might be asked misleading questions, and if in the interests of honesty he hesitated about answering, he could be made to seem unsure or evasive. In one murder trial where insanity was raised, the prosecutor hoped to prove that the defendant felt regret for his act and, hence, was aware that it was wrong; during his cross-examination of a defense psychiatrist, the following interchange took place:

Q: So I ask you, sir, in your opinion . . . was he or did he indicate in any way that he was sorry that he killed this girl?

A: He did not say he was sorry he had killed this girl and he was expecting the electric chair.

Q: Doctor. Can't you answer that question Yes or No?

A: I can only answer it on the basis of what I observed. I observed that . . .

Q: What is your opinion, doctor? Was he or was he not sorry that he killed the girl?

A: My opinion is that he regretted killing the girl but somehow felt it was in the cards, that something like this was going to happen in his life, and that he had no control over it, and this is the way it was going to be, he was going to get the chair and here it comes.

Q: So your answer is, doctor, that in your opinion from your examination of him he was sorry that he killed the girl? That is true, isn't it?

A: I would say he was sorry but felt there was nothing he could do about it.

Q: Doctor, are you trying to hedge on the answer?

A: I am trying to give you an accurate answer as to what I felt was going on in this man's mind.[3]

Some of this courtroom mudslinging and sanctioned harass-
ment was the unavoidable accompaniment to an adversarial
trial procedure, and though the imprecise nature of psychiatric
testimony rendered it more susceptible to certain forms of
attack than that of other experts, it was possible to foresee
and counteract many harmful effects. A competent defense
attorney could elicit full explanations from his witness on
direct examination, and if the prosecutor then tripped up,
distorted, or cut short the expert's statements, defense counsel
could bring out corrections, additions, and nuances in the
course of redirect examination.

There were, however, other problems that psychiatrists
claimed could make it nearly impossible for them to present
honest and meaningful testimony under any circumstances. A
witness's testimony is restricted, not only by the questions and
interruptions of opposing counsel, but by the law under which
he testifies and the scope of the issue his expertise is supposed
to address. A court that adhered closely to the letter of the
McNaughton Rule could restrict the flow of psychiatric testimony to the narrow and medically objectionable issue of
"knowledge of right and wrong." In theory, if the questions
or responses strayed far from this concise topic, the evidence
could be disallowed as irrelevant. Psychiatry had made phe-
nomenal progress since the days of Isaac Ray, and it seemed
somewhat absurd to force experts to testify under a rule which
even then had been considered anachronistic.

The question asked of us is monotonously the same: Did
the defendant know the nature and quality of the act and if
he did, did he know that it was wrong? The crux of the
question revolves around the word "know." The law automatically assumes that a child committing a felony does not
know the nature and quality of the act and does not know
that it is wrong. Yet a child of moderate brightness will say
that he hit his sister on the head, that she bled and then she

fell; he will even admit that she died or that he killed her and will perhaps say that he was wrong to kill his sister. The criminal code does not accept this knowledge as valid; without knowing it the law itself recognizes here a fundamental medico-psychological distinction between the purely verbal knowledge which characterizes the child and the other type of knowledge which characterizes the adult. This fundamental difference between verbal or purely intellectual knowledge and the mysterious other kind of knowledge is familiar to every clinical psychiatrist; it is the difference between knowledge divorced from affect and knowledge so fused with affect that it becomes a human reality.[4]

What the law clearly recognized about the child, however, it did not extend to the issue of mental illness, and the psychiatric witness was obliged to insinuate it by constructing his testimony to suit the requirements of the law. A psychiatrist who did not feel that he knew about the defendant's knowledge of right and wrong, or who felt that this was a moral issue which he was not qualified to evaluate, or who believed it altogether irrelevant to the really crucial question, might nonetheless say when he got to the stand that the defendant did not know the difference between right and wrong. He might say so knowing full well that the defendant *did* know the difference between right and wrong, having decided, on a medical or moral basis, that the defendant still lacked the mental wherewithal to be responsible for his acts, and that the medical evidence should convey this impression. In doing so he was simultaneously overstepping his role as a witness and committing perjury in order to achieve what he considered a proper verdict in spite of the law.

The courts often tended to agree with the psychiatrists, but the widespread recognition that the McNaughton Rule was somewhat arbitrary was more than counterbalanced by a fear that complete anarchy might result if the right-wrong test were broadened. When the possibility of abandoning Mc-Naughton was discussed in the course of the British Royal Commission on Capital Punishment's hearings in the early 1950s, jurists protested that there was sufficient practical elasticity in the application of the rules that neither defendants nor witnesses suffered unduly under them. The general feeling was that the judicial interpretation of McNaughton had grown ever more liberal over the years, perhaps to the point that " 'interpretation' might occasionally mean that the words were twisted into a meaning that could not reasonably be put on them, or even that the Rules might be ignored altogether."[5] The Director of Public Prosecutions opined that though British law expressly excluded irresistible impulse, it often crept in under the aegis of the vague "nature and quality of the act" clause of McNaughton—a phrase, in fact, that he thought often left "the jury untrammelled to use their common sense in looking at the facts of the particular case."[6] Both in England and in America it was believed that if a man was truly insane, the procedure would contrive to have him acquitted, and it little mattered what the rule happened to be. Why, then, should one change it and swap errors one had learned to live with for new and untried mistakes?

There were members of the bench and bar, however, who objected to this flagrant hypocrisy. "I think that to have rules which cannot be rationally justified except by a process of interpretation which distorts and often practically nullifies them . . . is not a desirable system," U.S. Supreme Court Justice Felix Frankfurter told the British commission. "I am a great believer in being as candid as possible about my institutions. They are in a large measure abandoned in practice, and therefore I think the M'Naghten Rules are very difficult for conscientious people and not difficult enough for people who say 'We'll just juggle them.' "[7]

For the law to be proud of self-violation was an absurd perversion of justice, and though it was claimed that the procedure negated McNaughton's improprieties, the combination of a rigid rule with anarchistic interpretation made it nearly impossible to guarantee any sort of consistent results. If it was desirable to have psychiatric testimony in criminal cases, the most rational approach seemed through civilized communication, without the formalities and falsehoods. As Dr. Bernard Diamond once suggested, an ideal court might say to the expert witness who appeared before it:

> Forget about the legal definitions and the technicalities; forget about sanity and insanity; premeditation, malice, and *mens rea*—that is our concern. Tell us everything that you, as a medical expert, know about this defendant. What kind of a person is he? What is wrong with him emotionally and mentally? How did he get to be the way he is now? What made him do what he is accused of? What hidden mechanisms in his mind caused him to behave in the way he did? What kind of treatment does he need to ensure his rehabilitation? Is he likely to respond to treatment? What kind of protection does society require to prevent something like this happening again? Tell us all that you know about this defendant, and we will give full consideration to what you have said; we will put it together with all the evidence from other sources: then we will decide what is best for society to do with this defendant.[8]

In 1949 David L. Bazelon was appointed judge in the U.S. Court of Appeals for the District of Columbia. After his prior experience in the tax division of a U.S. Attorney's office, his sudden exposure to Washington's criminal cases came as something of a shock. Looking back almost three decades later,[9] he says that he was baffled and fascinated by the stream of

defendants who came before his court. He took the liberty of
looking back through District Court files, transcripts, and pre-
sentence reports in search of some insight on these cases, and
concluded to his dismay that 90 percent of the defendants
were from an emotional, social, and intellectual background
utterly different from and almost incomprehensible to those
who made and administered the law. Yet they were tried and
sentenced without concern for the hidden causes and motiva-
tions behind their acts; the prevailing apathetic sentiment was
that the answer to crime was more prisons and longer sentences.
Judge Bazelon was particularly appalled when, following one
case where the convicted defendant had a tested I.Q. of 65—
in the mental defective range—he asked a respected colleague
on the bench whether it did not bother him, seem somehow
wrong, to find this poor wretch guilty of evil intent and trundle
him off to jail. "You know," said the colleague, inured to the
system, "you just can't excuse people for being dumb. A 65
I.Q., that's dumb."[10]

Looking back now, Judge Bazelon says that he chose to
tackle the insanity defense not as an end in itself, but as a
point of departure. He believed that the courtroom was one
of the most perfect social laboratories available, presenting a
unique opportunity to look in upon a man's life and ask not
only "Did he commit this crime?" but, if so, also "Why did
he do it?" "How did he come to this?" and "What can we do
to prevent this from happening again?" The insanity defense
made it possible to admit evidence on mental state, in however
limited a form, and to bring in behavioral experts to explain
the defendant's life. Ultimately one might hope to expand this
practice beyond cases of severe mental illness, and change the
philosophical underpinnings of the entire criminal justice
system so that each defendant could be approached as a unique
individual.

Bazelon was aware of the current restrictions on the insanity
defense, and of the psychiatrists' lament that the artificial

constraints of the McNaughton Rule hamstrung their contributions to the judicial process. Judge Bazelon therefore decided that reform of the insanity defense was essential, and made it known to the court's chief justice that he was interested in cases relating to this issue. He considered a number of potential test cases and encouraged defense counsel to work up detailed briefs on two of them. One was a capital case, which he ultimately rejected out of fear that the issue of capital punishment would confuse and overshadow the issue of insanity; the other was that of Monte Durham, who had been arrested on a simple housebreaking charge. According to Judge Bazelon's summary of Durham's life history:

Durham has a long history of imprisonment and hospitalization. In 1945, at the age of 17, he was discharged from the Navy after a psychiatric examination had shown that he suffered "from a profound personality disorder which renders him unfit for Naval service." In 1947 he pleaded guilty to violating the National Motor Theft Act and was placed on probation for one to three years. He attempted suicide, was taken to Gallinger Hospital for observation, and was transferred to St. Elizabeths Hospital, from which he was discharged after two months. In January of 1948, as a result of a conviction in the District of Columbia Municipal Court for passing bad checks, the District Court revoked his probation and he commenced service of his Motor Theft sentence. His conduct within the first few days in jail led to a lunacy inquiry in the Municipal Court where a jury found him to be of unsound mind. Upon commitment to St. Elizabeths, he was diagnosed as suffering from "psychosis with psychopathic personality." After 15 months of treatment, he was discharged in July 1949 as "recovered" and was returned to jail to serve the balance of his sentence. In June 1950 he was conditionally released. He violated the conditions by leaving the District. When he learned of a warrant for his arrest as a parole violator, he fled to the "South and Midwest obtaining money by passing a number of bad checks." After he was found and returned to the District, the Parole Board referred him to the District Court for a lunacy inquisition, wherein a jury again found him to be of unsound mind. He was readmitted to St. Elizabeths in February 1951. This time the diagnosis was "without mental disorder, psychopathic personality." He was discharged for the third time in May 1951.[11]

Two months after his release, on July 13, 1951, the police caught Monte Durham rifling an apartment. When they entered, he was cowering in a corner with a T-shirt over his head, and about $50 worth of property in his pockets. Due to his psychiatric history and the fact that, according to his mother, he had suffered from hallucinations following his May discharge from St. Elizabeths, he was given a mental examination. Two psychiatrists found that he suffered from "psychosis with psychopathic personality," and he was again committed. After sixteen months he was released to the District Jail as competent to stand trial.

Durham raised a defense of insanity, but the court refused to admit it and he was convicted. Under a previous ruling[12] it had been said that defendants were presumed to be sane until and unless "some evidence of mental disorder" was introduced, at which point insanity became an issue that the prosecution had the burden of refuting. The court did not feel that the evidence presented in Durham's case was sufficient to topple this presumption, a decision that the appellate court held to have been prejudicial error. The sole psychiatric witness had stated on four occasions that Durham was "of unsound mind" before, after, and during the crime; Durham's mother's testimony indicated an abnormal fear of people; and Durham's own testimony was sometimes incoherent. The trial court had decided that this constituted "no testimony" rather than "some testimony" because the question of insanity at the time of the crime was not adequately covered, and because the expert witness's testimony referred to "unsoundness of mind" without addressing the McNaughton question of capacity to distinguish between right and wrong. In fact, the doctor had been a particularly cautious witness, unwilling to say more than he knew, and when asked whether the defendant "knew the difference between right and wrong in connection with governing his own actions," had replied:

> Dr. Gilbert: . . . I don't know how anyone can answer that question categorically, except as one's experience leads him to know that most mental cases can give you a categorical answer of right and wrong, but what influence these symptoms have on abnormal behavior or anti-social behavior—
> The Court: Well, your answer is that you are unable to form an opinion, is that it?
> Dr. Gilbert: I would say that that is essentially true, for the reasons that I have given.[13]

When defense counsel sought elaboration on this point by Dr. Gilbert, the court interrupted, saying that the witness had already answered the question.

Durham's conviction was reversed and the case remanded on these grounds alone,° but defense counsel's appeal had also questioned the adequacy of the prevailing District of Columbia test of insanity, which had been the right-wrong rule since 1886, supplemented by irresistible impulse since 1929. Judge Bazelon took this opportunity to change that rule.

° Monte Durham was retried under the "Durham Rule," convicted of housebreaking and petty larceny, and sentenced to one to four years. This conviction was reversed on appeal because the trial judge, in his instructions to the jury, mentioned that if acquitted by reason of insanity Durham would remain in a hospital until he was "of sound mind," and, he added, prejudicing the case, "if the authorities adhered to their last opinion on this point, he will be released very shortly." At his third trial, Durham pleaded guilty.

The new formulation that Bazelon ordered be applied in Durham's retrial and in all future cases was a simple construction nearly identical to the New Hampshire Rule:

"An accused is not criminally responsible if his unlawful act was the product of mental disease or defect."[14]

A "mental disease" in this sense was "a condition which is considered capable of either improving or deteriorating"; a "mental defect" one "not considered capable of either improving or deteriorating and which may be either congenital, or the result of injury, or the residual effect of a physical or mental disease."[15]

In the judicial debates following McNaughton's case, Justice Maule had objected to the precise wording of the rules, and correctly anticipated that the words themselves might hinder the future course of justice. Judge Bazelon took care to avoid this in the *Durham* decision, stating that "[w]e do not, and indeed could not, formulate an instruction which would be either appropriate or binding in all cases."[16] Instead, he suggested that however the instructions were phrased, they should convey the idea that, once some evidence of insanity had been raised, unless it was proved beyond a reasonable doubt that there was no mental disease or defect, or that there was no causal relationship between such disease or defect and commission of the criminal act, the jury must acquit. The presence of mental illness alone was not sufficient; it must be causally related to the crime, but the nature of this causation was a question for the jury to determine based upon the expert testimony and the facts of the case.

"The essential error of M'Naghten," Bazelon wrote some years later,

and of tests like it which attach a great many qualifications to the term "mental disease," is that it demands information more precise than any we can reasonably supply at this time. When psychiatry—and other behavioral sciences—

have advanced to the point where they can unequivocally identify the springs of responsibility, then and only then will we be able to justify some narrow definition of insanity. But we are in that long period known as "meanwhile." So meanwhile it seems to me far preferable that we use phrases and words most likely to accommodate an expanding body of knowledge to the requirements of each case which arises.[17]

Eager, as Judge Doe had been, to reassure the conservative legal community that he was not making new law out of whole cloth, Bazelon assured jurists, on the one hand, that *Durham* was directly based upon the New Hampshire Rule and, on the other hand, that *Durham* did not put an unreasonable demand on the jury, because the questions it asked were precisely analogous to those routinely given to juries in tort cases. In a negligence suit the jury might be asked to determine whether the respondent had exercised that degree of care to be expected of a "reasonable man of ordinary prudence," and in disability claims juries are regularly asked, based upon conflicting medical testimony, to evaluate the degree of the plaintiff's disability. They were difficult questions, but juries had always been able to handle them without specific tests and rules.

Psychiatrists widely praised the *Durham* decision as the major breakthrough that finally sounded the death knell of the McNaughton Rule and would permit them at last to contribute what they knew. Many jurists agreed. Bazelon believed he had opened the courtroom doors to psychiatry, but years later, when the *Durham* experiment was over, he would complain that it did no good. And while this door was ajar, a series of grotesqueries came in, some the result of the agitated pushing and testing inevitable whenever there is a change in the law, others related more fundamentally to the specific changes made.

The earliest difficulties encountered by *Durham* were almost identical to its advantages, namely, the lack of precise terms, tests, or rules. Judge Bazelon's working definitions of "mental disease" and "mental defect" distinguished each from the other but, as intended, avoided distinguishing either from anything else. But stripped of all tests and qualifications, these terms seemed very vague indeed, even though they were critical determiners of the trial's outcome. Under the Mc-Naughton Rule the emphasis was less on the presence or absence of something called mental disease than on whether or not this mental state, whatever it was called, precluded the capacity to distinguish right from wrong. Under the *Durham* formulation, figuring out whether or not there was a "mental disease or defect" was already half the battle, and jurors were understandably eager to know what these things were.

Attempts on the part of trial judges to define mental disease or defect for juries, however, were discouraged by the D.C. Circuit Court of Appeals. The issue first arose in *Stewart* v. *United States*,[18] an appeal of a first-degree murder conviction decided two weeks after *Durham.* During Stewart's trial there had been expert testimony that he suffered from a psychopathic personality, but the trial judge altered the significance of this evidence by intimating in his instructions to the jury that a psychopathic personality was a "disorder" rather than a "disease" or a "defect," and that only physical deterioration or damage to the brain could warrant an insanity acquittal. The court of appeals reversed on grounds that it was not up to the judge to set bounds on the insanity defense: it was the right of the jury alone to determine which types and degrees of mental abnormality entitled the defendant to acquittal.

There was similar ambiguity about the other critical *Durham* term, "product." In the loosest sense, one could say that mental illness tinges all aspects of the thought process of the sufferer, and that his every act is at least partially affected by mental disease, but such flaccid reasoning would drain the word "product" of all meaning. At the other extreme one could demand that there be a very direct and obvious causality

This rather unsatisfying and impenetrable collection of synonyms and cautions was the farthest the court of appeals was willing to go in guiding the jury since, as it reaffirmed in the same decision, the jury alone was to make the inferences from the facts and reach the ultimate conclusions without the judicial meddling which for so long was supposed to have hampered the free flow of expert testimony. Moreover, the jury was encouraged to reach wherever it needed for information, and the court took care to mention that not only psychiatrists but lay witnesses, were entitled to testify on the issue of insanity, since mental illness is evidenced by abnormal behavior and lay people are fully qualified to speak of departures from normalcy.

It was very exciting to think of this hypothetical *Durham* jury—twelve randomly selected citizens given the heavy burden not merely of passing judgment on an indicted felon, but of understanding a fellow human being and learning why he behaved as he did. They were asked to determine subtle issues of psychiatric cause and effect and to sort through moral issues at a level quite outside a layman's normal realm of experience. It was a difficult task, but they would be helped by the witnesses: scientists of the human mind would dissect and display the inner workings of the defendant with all the accumulated knowledge of their field. It was as though one hoped to reeducate society, twelve people at a time. Above all, in each case it would ultimately be the jurors' new understanding and innate sense of social justice that would determine the verdict rather than an artificially constructed rule or the beliefs of a single profession.

Unfortunately, theory and practice soon parted ways, and it became evident that when the court renounced its tight McNaughton control over the insanity issue, it was abdicating not, as hoped, in favor of the jury, but in favor of the experts. Quite often after the psychiatric witnesses had addressed the two critical issues of the existence of mental disease or defect and their causal relationship to the act, there was very little left for the jury to decide, and their sacrosanct right to make all inferences and reach the ultimate conclusion became little more than a right of rubber stamp approval.

The most dramatic examples of this were results of the District of Columbia's stance on the burden of proof, which was that once the initial presumption of sanity had been toppled by some evidence of the defendant's mental illness, the burden shifted onto the prosecution to prove that the defendant was sane at the time of the crime. Quite often, a prosecutor faced with a less than persuasive insanity defense will, for strategic reasons, choose not to call his own psychiatric experts; rather than dignifying the defendant's claim of insanity by fighting it on medical grounds, he will refute it through lay testimony and through cross-examination of the defense psychiatrists. In the early years of *Durham*, however, this strategy had a curious result.

Between 1956 and 1962 there were several cases where the defense called experts who testified that the defendant was mentally ill and that his criminal act was the product of his illness—assertions that the prosecution refuted through lay testimony. The earliest case[20] is typical: two defense psychiatrists appeared, one said that the defendant suffered from psychosis, the other that he had dementia praecox and, when asked about its causal relationship to the crime, stated, "It contributed largely to it, I would say, by reason of the serious nature of the disease." The prosecutor called only lay witnesses, who said that the defendant had behaved perfectly normally. After listening to the evidence, making its inferences, reaching its ultimate conclusion, the jury discounted the expert testimony and convicted the defendant. The verdict, however, was reversed on appeal because, it was said, the prosecution had not successfully refuted the defense's medical testimony on insanity and hence had not met its burden of proof, and consequently the jury *could not* have found the defendant guilty through a proper application of the law. The "ultimate conclusion" had dwindled almost to nothing.

The situation was aggravated by the fact that, in the absence of any legal or operational definition of "mental disease or defect," psychiatric witnesses quite naturally tended to equate the terms with medical ones. No court anywhere had ever wished to excuse every criminal with a diagnosable mental disorder, but this is what threatened to occur, and the witnesses' conclusions were less susceptible to cross-examination than ever before. Theoretically if a psychiatrist said the defendant suffered from paranoid schizophrenia, the most the prosecutor could do to question this statement directly would be to ask, "And is that *really* a mental disease or defect?" Some critics suggested that according to the *Durham* court's logic, a defendant with migraine or "psychophysiological gastrointes-tinal reaction," or psychosomatic heartburn, should be able to topple the presumption of sanity and shift the burden of proof to the prosecutor, since these ailments had medical names and appeared in the *Diagnostic and Statistical Manual*'s list of mental disorders. During one case appealed on few other grounds than a purely semantic argument over whether or not an "emotionally unstable personality" was or was not a mental disease, Judge Warren Burger, then a member of the D.C. Circuit Court of Appeals and one of *Durham*'s most adamant critics, said that in the worst of cases it might be necessary only for the defendant himself to take the stand, murmur, "I've always been emotionally unstable,"[21] and then sit back while the prosecutor writhed under the burden of disproving this assertion beyond a reasonable doubt.

In one dreadful homicide case, the entire trial outcome did seem to hinge on a mere choice of words and nothing more. In 1957, Comer Blocker[22] was convicted for the murder of his common-law wife despite his plea of insanity. Three psy-chiatrists had testified: one said that nothing was wrong with him, the other two said he suffered from a "sociopathic personality disturbance," though both agreed that this was not classified as a mental disease. Blocker was convicted in October. In November, two senior staff members of St. Elizabeths Hospital determined that, for purely administrative reasons, sociopathy would henceforth be categorized as a mental disease. Blocker appealed his conviction on grounds of this "new medical evidence"—i.e., that the condition he had always had was now a mental disease. The conviction was reversed.

Judge Burger filed several lengthy opinions criticizing the fact that *Durham* had permitted the expert witness to usurp the role of the jury and run free with the verdict. As he commented elsewhere:

> I have heard psychiatrists frankly say that if they conclude that their patient is ill and in need of treatment, they consider it their professional obligation to try to make certain that he goes to a mental institution rather than a prison, even if it is necessary to "tailor" their expert testimony to accomplish that end.[23]

Understandable this may have been, and even praiseworthy, but the law is constructed by legislators and judges elected and appointed by the collective citizenry, and ought not to be given over to one subspecialty whose beliefs and reasoning, however enlightened and benevolent, are independent of social control. Yet psychiatric testimony was becoming unassailable on any grounds other than psychiatric. The insanity defense was going haywire under *Durham*, and it appeared to be due to a psychiatric dictatorship combined with procedural anarchy rather than to any change in jurors' views or reeducation of society. The statistics were quite alarming. Whereas in 1954, the year *Durham* was decided, 0.4 percent of the cases tried in Washington's U.S. District Court ended in a finding of NGRI—close to the national average—by the following year the figure had quadrupled, to 1.8 percent. In

1958 it was 3.3 percent; in 1959, 6.1 percent; in 1960, 8.8 percent; and finally in 1961 the figure rocketed up to 14.4 percent. One out of every seven defendants was being found not guilty by reason of insanity.[24]

Judge Bazelon himself was growing thoroughly disenchanted with the effects of *Durham.* He had meant to open the courtroom door to psychiatry, he said, not to hand psychiatrists the key. Moreover, he felt he had been led up the garden path by psychiatrists who had rattled their McNaughton chains for years, complaining that no one would let them speak, but who ended up having remarkably little to say. At least under the McNaughton Rule witnesses had to grapple with the test and to explain their medical reasoning in terms of "knowledge of right and wrong," which, however artificial and misleading, was at least comprehensible to the jurors. Under *Durham,* they tended to abuse their new freedom and to testify in technical, conclusory, and ultimately useless terms. No sooner did expert witnesses approach a topic of potential utility to the jurors than the issues were distracted and obscured by uninformative bickering over whether the defendant's condition should be characterized as a "personality defect," a "personality problem," a "personality disorder," a "disease," an "illness," or just a plain old "type of personality."[25] "Even if these labels had meaning for the witnesses, the testimony was useless unless that meaning was communicated to the jury."[26]

In one bitter commentary, Bazelon's court expressed doubt that even the experts knew what their jargon meant, since when challenged, they proved remarkably poor at explaining it to anyone else. The court cited one psychiatrist's attempt to tell the jury what he meant when he said the defendant had a "passive-aggressive personality":

> [It] is a type of personality that an individual has, that is, everybody has some type of personality. We all have a type of personality. I mean no one has no personality. We have

93

some type. Well, you may say schizoid personality, or compulsive personality, but speaking of the one that you ask, such [as] the passive aggressive personality, these are broken down into two different categories.

One is passive and one is aggressive. Usually in these people the aggressive type acts out in an aggressive manner, to either major or minor stressful situations, they maneuver under close confinement or under strict rules and regulations except maneuvering into a psychosis.

It is generally considered that the passive type or the aggressive type frequently or sometimes an aggressive personality will also behave in a passive manner.

This is where we get the term "passive-aggressive." This is more a classification of the type of personality that the individual has.[27]

From 1961 on, the D.C. Circuit Court of Appeals began wresting control back from psychiatrists. The 1962 *McDonald* decision[28] overtly stated that "[w]hat psychiatrists may consider a 'mental disease or defect' for clinical purposes, where their concern is treatment, may or may not be the same as mental disease or defect for the jury's purpose in determining criminal responsibility."[29] The court went on, contrary to the original intent of *Durham,* to provide some working definition of the terms "mental disease or defect" as "any abnormal condition of the mind which substantially affects mental or emotional processes and substantially impairs behavior controls."[30] This new *Durham-McDonald* test gave the issue back to the jury by giving them some adverbs to work on: whatever the psychiatrists said, the jury always had some room to consider whether or not the effect or impairment had really been *substantial.*

There continued to be cases where convicted defendants demanded a directed verdict in their favor because the prosecution had not met its burden of proof, but the court of appeals was now disinclined to reverse, thus reaffirming the jury's attenuated right to decide independently of expert witnesses. Eventually the court of appeals prohibited psychiatrists from testifying on the ultimate questions at all. Experts could no longer say whether the act was the "product" of illness, and though they were still permitted to use the words "mental disease" and "mental defect," they were strongly encouraged to avoid the use of technical labels. Psychiatrists were reminded that they were present in the courtroom to help understand the defendant, not to seize control of the trial. Judge Bazelon suggested that expert witnesses be instructed that they should not concern themselves with the issue of criminal responsibility at all, since it was outside the realm of their expertise. What they should say was what they knew. "What is desired in this case is the kind of opinion you would give to a family which brought one of its members to your clinic and asked for your diagnosis of his mental condition and a description of how his condition would be likely to influence his conduct."[31]

In a footnote to one opinion, Judge Bazelon pessimistically observed that even these instructions might not help, and that possibly, after all, "psychiatry and the other social and behavioral sciences cannot provide sufficient data relevant to a determination of criminal responsibility no matter what our rules of evidence are."[32] In this event, it might be necessary to eliminate the insanity defense, or at least to divorce it from medical theories.

Finally, in 1972, the *Durham* experiment ended altogether, not due to dramatic new difficulties, but due rather to the accumulation of eighteen years of problems and patchwork solutions and, above all, to simple exasperation. The experiment had admittedly failed, though the very magnitude of its failure made it a spectacular success, since the controversies over *Durham* and the interest it sparked in both legal and psychiatric circles caused more studies to be made, more papers to be written, and more law to be refashioned than had been done in the preceding century.

The test that Judge Bazelon's court adopted in place of *Durham-McDonald*[33] was that proposed in the American Law Institute's Model Penal Code in 1955, and which had since been adopted in many states and all but one of the other federal circuit courts. The American Law Institute is a private organization dedicated to the improvement of the law, whose scholars have, over the decades, compiled careful "restatements" of the law, among them the Model Penal Code, which attempts to integrate the criminal justice system according to the most reasonable and generally accepted principles. It happened that the ALI was considering the issue of criminal responsibility just at the time when Bazelon's court instituted the *Durham* rule, but the institute rejected the *Durham* formula, correctly anticipating problems that the unqualified "product" rule would incur.[34]

The code's authors believed that the McNaughton formulation was essentially correct as far as it went, since it expressed the issue of insanity not merely within a medical context, but in proper terms of whether or not the defendant was susceptible to the restraining influence of the law and whether he possessed the sort of guilty mind which the penal system was supposed to punish, rehabilitate, or deter. The major flaw was in not going quite far enough and in tying the rule to a strictly cognitive model expressed in ambiguous words. It had always been unclear, for example, whether the word "know" merely meant to be capable of verbalizing an awareness, or whether it required some more profound psychological grasp of an action's significance and implications, and whether "wrong" denoted legal wrong or a more inclusive sense of moral wrong. Many jurisdictions had seen a need to supplement McNaughton with the irresistible impulse clause, while many of the rest, without adopting that test, had broadened their interpretation of McNaughton's words to accommodate the concept.

The American Law Institute's Model Penal Code test, more commonly known as the ALI rule, was no more than a linguistically modernized version of McNaughton plus irresistible impulse, stating that:

A person is not responsible for criminal conduct if at the time of such conduct as a result of mental disease or defect he lacks substantial capacity either to appreciate the criminality of his conduct or to conform his conduct to the requirements of law.[35]°

It was a neat and concise formulation that skirted earlier verbal problems without significantly widening the scope of the insanity defense. For McNaughton jurisdictions whose case law was weighted down by a century of interpretations, ALI wiped the books clean, and set down an authoritative and uncontroversial, if rather bland, modern test.

The District of Columbia's change from *Durham-McDonald* to ALI made very little difference, since by then the rules were virtually identical in practice. The main reason for making the change, perhaps, was a wish to fall in line with the other circuit courts, and a feeling that the *Durham* debacle had lasted quite long enough, and that it was time to lay it to rest and move on to other things.

° A second portion of the ALI test states: "The terms 'mental disease or defect' do not include an abnormality manifested only by repeated criminal or otherwise anti-social conduct." This section was included because there were mental health specialists who said that psychopathy or sociopathy was a mental disease, but one whose primary or even sole feature was a persistent disregard for legal and social restrictions. Though the ALI rule was not intended to exclude psychopaths categorically, one could not excuse someone from guilt *only* because he committed crimes.

7

THE JURY AND THE
INSANITY DEFENSE

During *Durham*'s reign, and only partly because of it, not only the D.C. Circuit Court of Appeals, but nearly everyone, suddenly grew weary of the ancient debate over which test of insanity should be used. In curious contrast to their earlier point of view, both psychiatrists and lawyers seemed to decide that it had never really been the test itself that made presentation of psychiatric testimony so unpleasant, but inherent aspects of courtroom procedure, or even, perhaps, the witnesses' own expectation that the rule would limit what they could say.

Abraham Goldstein, former dean of the Yale Law School, once Judge Bazelon's law clerk, and author of a standard work on the insanity defense, stated in 1967 that "there is virtually no support in law for the view that *M'Naghten* is responsible for inhibiting the flow of testimony on the insanity issue. . . . The almost unvarying policy of the courts has been to admit *any* evidence of aberrational behavior so long as it is probative of the defendant's mental condition, without regard to the supposed restrictions of the test used to define insanity for the jury."[1] By way of illustration he cited a case where a judge admitted a father's testimony that his son, the defendant, "was a pale, delicate boy from birth and disposed to be melancholic" on grounds that this information contributed to an understanding of the defendant's mental state.

A 1970 American Bar Foundation survey similarly found that psychiatric evidence was limited or excluded only when witnesses "were clearly rambling or where testimony was irrelevant in a commonsensical view of legal relevancy."[2] No prosecutors, defense attorneys, psychiatrists, or judges interviewed in the course of the project could recall a single case where testimony had been restricted, and the consensus was that if courts erred at all it was in the direction of admitting far too much expert testimony.

Supplementing this impression that tests were not as harmful as previously supposed was the growing sentiment that they did not help as much, either, and that the subtle distinctions in wording that were the topics of such heated debate aimed at a degree of perfection that could never be achieved in the real world of a courtroom. The purpose of *Durham* had been to introduce an unprecedented array and depth of evidence that was theoretically ideal but which might, in practice, be more detailed than a jury could find useful. As law professor Ralph Slovenko comments, reflecting upon Judge Bazelon's hopes for the *Durham* rule:

The question is, what did he want? Norman Mailer wrote a very good book on Gary Gilmore, *The Executioner's Song.* He gave a very good description of Gilmore; you almost get tired of reading about Gary Gilmore at the end, but you get a full picture. Now if you could write a long report like that for every defendant who came before the court, would the judge read it? Would the jury want it? What do you need to know? What is important? When I was working on a construction job one summer when I was in college, the engineer had the plans for the laying of a sewer pipe specified to an eighth of an inch. But when you got out there in the field, and started digging, you were lucky if you were within three inches. You just couldn't do it with the shovel and the mud. You couldn't do it, and it's the same way with the court. After all, what are the dispositional things that the court can do? It can send him to prison, or send him to the hospital, or put him on probation, and what is it you need to know to make that decision? Do you need to know that the person had a poor upbringing, that he masturbated as a child? Just what is it that you need to know?[3]

Throughout the years both legal and medical men had criticized the prevailing system, and held up cases where insane men were convicted or vicious fiends were acquitted as exemplifying the unfortunate effects of a bad rule. It was a curious phenomenon that these critics themselves always knew who should be held responsible or not responsible, and needed only to find some rule under which everyone else would arrive at the same conclusion. If the jurors "erred," it was because the insanity test perverted the choices, or because the psychiatric evidence was stunted or twisted until they didn't know what they should think. No one ever thought to ask the jurors themselves what they thought of the insanity test, or what problems they had with the rules and the testimony, because even though, in an abstract sense, the jury is viewed as the most admirable representation of our democratic system of justice, jurors themselves are too often seen as sheep and imbeciles to be herded back and forth by opposing lawyers. While, on the one hand, courts repeatedly insisted that the ultimate decision was to be made by the jury, the courts were always careful to keep the scope of that decision within acceptable bounds. Under the original ALI rule the key decision for the jury to make was whether a defendant's lack of capacity was "substantial," and the courts were able to indicate fairly precisely what they expected "substantial" to mean. When the American Law Institute proposed an alternative formulation stating that a defendant would not be criminally responsible if, due to mental disease or defect, "his capacity either to appreciate the criminality of his conduct or to conform his conduct to the requirements of law is so substantially impaired *that he cannot justly be held responsible*"[4]*—a formula that Judge Bazelon recommended to replace *Durham*—courts rejected it from fear of what might happen if juries were allowed to run wild with their own sense of justice.

Occasionally juries do run away with the law. One hears of cases during Prohibition where jurors listened while an ironclad case was built around an innocuous, small-scale bootlegger, and returned with a verdict of not guilty. Some tax violation cases are difficult to prosecute because jurors feel little sympathy for the victimized Internal Revenue Service. Insanity cases are often a particularly ripe area for jury discretion, since jurors are free, on the one hand, sympathetically to interpret a wide range of emotional stress as "insanity," or, at the other extreme, to dismiss much flagrantly bizarre behavior as mere manifestations of a warped and vicious mind.

Harry K. Thaw was one example of a man who was acquitted by reason of the jury's sympathy. A 1927 Ohio case furnishes another striking example. George Remus, a former soda jerk, druggist, patent medicine manufacturer, quack doctor, lawyer, and, following Prohibition, millionaire bootlegger with twenty-nine prison sentences on his résumé, was charged with shooting his wife to death as she entered a Cincinnati courthouse to divorce him. Three hours later, Remus told a psychiatrist that he was not crazy, never had been crazy, and would not use the insanity defense, but at the end of ten days he changed his mind and claimed to suffer from "transitory maniacal insanity," a medically dubious diagnosis which, oddly enough, he had already invoked as a practicing lawyer when defending a uxoricidal client thirteen years earlier.

* Emphasis added.

As Harry K. Thaw had done, George Remus conducted much of his defense through the newspapers, which readily printed his unsubstantiated allegations that his wife had been having an affair, and his scarcely credible suggestion that her lover had conspired to have him killed. Many of the rumors were demonstrably false, but this did not lessen their effectiveness. Despite the flimsiness of the medical testimony at the trial, it took the jury only nineteen minutes to return with a verdict of not guilty by reason of insanity, or rather, as the dean of the Ohio State University Law School put it, with a verdict "that Mrs. Remus was guilty."[5]

Again, as with Thaw, the initial public jubilation at the acquittal of a wronged husband who had killed in legitimate defense of honor rapidly turned sour. The jurors, who publicly said that they had chosen an insanity acquittal at the December 20 trial "in order to let him out for a happy Christmas at last"[6] were soon held up as shining examples of gullible laymen easily led astray by high-paid psychiatrists and nimble-tongued lawyers. Prosecutor Charles Taft II, son of the former President, who was at this time Chief Justice of the United States, called for immediate and radical reform of the insanity laws, and a committee of the National Crime Commission, under the chairmanship of Theodore Roosevelt's daughter, strongly recommended taking the issue of insanity out of the hands of lay jurors and letting panels of professionals decide.[7]

Such highly publicized aberrances are the exception, however, and often one does not know whether to categorize unlikely acquittals as horrible miscarriages of justice or as instances where society's verdict, as expressed through the jury, stemmed from a sense of justice more profound than the law. Sometimes juries are misled, and sometimes they merely appear to be duped because their decisions rest upon quantities of evidence that breakfast-table jurors do not find in their morning newspapers. In most cases where a jury determines the question of insanity, the verdict follows in some plausible way from the facts. But by what process do jurors do this, and how tightly constrained are they by the rules and the testimony?

In the 1950s and 1960s several investigators undertook systematic and empirical research of the jury system.[8] Even most of those who began their investigations as cynics emerged with new respect for the nature and quality of jury deliberations and decisions, though the processes involved often appeared strikingly different from what the law assumed and planned. At the height of the *Durham* court's difficult struggle with test formulations, expert testimony, and the jury's autonomous power to decide, several researchers turned their attention specifically to the question of jurors and the insanity defense, and reached somewhat surprising conclusions.

In an effort to determine how well jurors might understand the precise wording and careful nuances of insanity tests, one study[9] exposed groups of Washington-area university undergraduates to actual *Durham* insanity instructions of various complexity and length, and then tested them for comprehension. Though these experimental subjects were not under the moral pressure of a real criminal trial, they were well-educated students, accustomed to absorbing information and repeating it under test conditions, and one could assume that their understanding would be at least as accurate as that of actual jurors.

The results of the test were appalling. By the experimenters' appraisal, only about a third of the subjects could repeat any reasonable approximation of the *Durham* rule, simple though it was. Asked to paraphrase the test, or to explain how severe mental disease or defect needed to be to justify an insanity acquittal, the students plucked diverse and peculiar elements from the instructions they had heard. "Mentally insane, such that the person is not reasoning or using his mind in the ordinary sense. 'He must be completely unreasonable, incapable of thinking.' " "A mental disease or defect for an insanity acquittal would have to be serious enough to color judgment."

"When the insane person is completely unconscious of what he is doing." "The defendant has to be proven beyond a reasonable doubt that he is insane or incapable of making decisions or caring for himself." Quite a surprising number of subjects, asked to summarize the *Durham* instructions they had just heard, wrote down a formula more similar to the McNaughton Rule; the judge's instructions sometimes mentioned inability to distinguish right from wrong as one possible manifestation of exculpatory mental disease, and this familiar and memorable catch phrase evidently stayed in the listeners' minds more readily than *Durham*'s ethereal notion of causality.

Jurors, the experimenters concluded, demonstrably did not understand the insanity instructions that the law had so carefully prepared and the judge so assiduously explained, nor could they carry any accurate memory of them from the courtroom to the deliberation chamber, and they were, as a consequence, "bound to fall back upon a jurisprudence of their own."[10] What exactly this ad hoc jurisprudence might be was not clear, though in general the conditions articulated by this population of college students were more restrictive than *Durham* was intended to be, and required dramatic impairment of cognitive functions.

In a more ambitious set of experiments run within the context of a major jury research project at the University of Chicago, Rita James Simon[11] attempted to determine what effect different jury instructions had on the final verdict, and how much difference it made if expert witnesses were permitted to testify in what they considered psychiatrically valid terms, unfettered by legal restraints. The experimental procedure more closely approximated actual trial conditions than had the Washington study. With the cooperation of courts in three cities, Simon obtained test panels from regular jury pools. Two real insanity cases were selected for the experiment: Monte Durham's housebreaking trial, and an incest case in which a man was accused of having sex with his two daughters over a period of fourteen years. The original trial transcripts were edited down to sixty- or ninety-minute minitrials, which were tape-recorded by volunteer actors. Specific segments of the recorded trials could then be changed, so that different juries could hear trials that were identical to the last word and inflection except for the critical element the experimenter wished to examine, such as the psychiatric testimony or the judge's instructions.

In the first phase of the experiment, juries sat through one of the "trials," then were given one of three sets of instructions: (1) the McNaughton right-wrong rule, (2) the *Durham* product rule, (3) an invented rule, categorized as "uninstructed," which hinged entirely on the question of mental illness without reference to either responsibility or causality: "If you believe the defendant was insane at the time he committed the act of which he is accused, then you must find the defendant not guilty by reason of insanity." The hope was to study the effect of the insanity test used on the verdict, though the experimental conditions were somewhat complicated by the fact that the recorded expert testimony had to be slightly different for each of the three cases. Experts testifying for the McNaughton juries discussed the defendant's knowledge of right and wrong, whereas those testifying under *Durham* addressed the question of productivity.

Given the evidence that juries do not fully grasp the insanity instructions in the first place, it is scarcely surprising that a change in instructions had far less effect on the verdict than legal scholars had always supposed. In the housebreaking case, where psychiatric testimony indicated that the defendant satisfied all three tests of insanity, the "uninstructed" group acquitted slightly more often, but there was no significant difference between the verdicts reached by McNaughton and *Durham* juries. The jurors' opinion of the defendant's responsibility was immune to changes in the test.

In the incest case, on the other hand, there were significant differences, though they were not entirely attributable to the jury's application of the instructions. Consulting psychiatrists told the experimenters that, given the psychopathology of the original defendant, an expert properly testifying under a strict McNaughton Rule would have to say that the defendant did know right from wrong and consequently was *not* legally insane, whereas an expert testifying under *Durham* should properly state that the act was the product of mental disease or defect and that therefore the defendant *was* legally insane. Whether a real expert witness, who would have formed his medical opinion of the defendant independently of legal tests, would so scrupulously have observed the semantic niceties when he got into court rather than tailoring his testimony to achieve a given end, is a matter for speculation. Nonetheless, under the experimental conditions, faced with different psychiatric conclusions and different sets of instructions, five of the twenty-six *Durham* juries found the defendant NGRI and six could not reach a verdict, whereas none of the twenty McNaughton juries acquitted, and there was a single hung jury.

Independent of the experimental trials, the jurors from all groups were told both the *Durham* test and the McNaughton Rule and asked which they, as people now experienced in deliberating the insanity issue, would prefer to see used in real-life trials. One third preferred McNaughton, one third preferred *Durham,* and the remaining third could not perceive enough difference between the two to warrant having any preference.

In another phase of the Simon experiment, juries were compared on the basis of the type of psychiatric testimony they heard. Some heard "typical" testimony, whether that actually presented at the original trial or a facsimile tailored to fit the instructions, while the others heard "model" testimony. In the model testimony there was more information about the defendant's life history, fuller clinical detail, explanations of all technical terms, and an attempt to elucidate fully the connection between the mental state and the criminal act. The psychiatrists who collaborated in writing the model testimony felt that it provided a very distinct and interesting contrast to the typical testimony, and believed that it was probably as lucid and complete as anyone could hope to find in a trial.

Sixty-eight juries heard the incest case, thirty-three with model testimony, thirty-five with typical testimony. Even though the earlier experiment had indicated that it was a case near the border of responsibility, in which one might assume that more complete and penetrating psychiatric explanations of the defendant's behavior would result in more insanity acquittals, there was no meaningful difference at all between the verdicts reached by the two groups. Perhaps more surprising to psychiatrists were the results of questionnaires asking for jurors' appraisals of the psychiatric testimony. The majority of jurors under both conditions found the testimony helpful, did not find it too technical, and did not want any further information from the experts. The typical group was every bit as satisfied as the model group.

If neither the wording of the test nor the general quality of the psychiatric testimony is the determiner of the outcome of a jury insanity trial, what does make the difference? One cannot really tell. For that matter, it is not at all clear how a trial outcome ever is determined: the most alarming bit of evidence demonstrated by the Simon study was completely incidental to the thrust of the research and passed unmentioned. Ten juries deliberated on the incest case under the *Durham* rule after hearing typical psychiatric testimony. For these juries the instructions were the same, the evidence was the same, every word that they heard was the same, each moment of their respective courtroom experiences was identical to the last detail, yet four of them voted NGRI, three convicted, and three were hung. As with the construction engineer designing a sewer ditch, theorists may aspire toward mathematical precision, but should recognize that when the jurors apply themselves to the task with the material and tools at hand, such precise theories will seem quite irrelevant.

Though one cannot say exactly what determines the outcome of a trial, one can isolate some of the considerations that jurors find important. In Simon's experiments, recordings were made of the jurors' deliberations, and she found that they were quite fully aware that they were not supposed merely to rubber-stamp the experts' diagnosis, but were to reach their own opinions about the defendant's insanity. Their conclusions hinged upon a view of mental illness that was rather naive from a modern psychiatric point of view, and even, perhaps, from the perspective of a nineteenth-century alienist, but which was in fairly close accord with popular conceptions of madmen and responsibility.

When discussing the incest case, the jurors found it to weigh against a verdict of insanity that the defendant was employed as a fireman and did his job well, that he had scored well on his civil service exam, been promoted twice, and supervised several men. The jurors needed evidence of some more fundamental perversion of his reasoning and functioning abilities if they were to find him insane, yet even in activities connected with his crime he had demonstrated awareness, intelligence, and planning. The defendant did not rape his daughters, nor were his sexual relations with them accompanied by violent outbursts or irrational behavior; on the contrary, he took precautions against being found out, and even thought always to use some form of contraception. These facts were more important to the jurors than the psychiatrists' expert testimony about "paraphiliac neurosis" and "unresolved oedipal tensions." As one juror deliberating under a *Durham* instruction remarked:

> The point is you can have a quirk and still be a member

of society as long as you have the mental sense not to allow your quirk to break the law. But, if you break the law, because you have this quirk and still have the mental capacity to know what you are doing and go ahead and do it deliberately, then you are not insane. Then it is no excuse or alibi that you have a quirk.[12]

Juries may not be very scientific, but they try very hard to be just.

Prosecutors and defense attorneys have empirically formed an image of jurors' views on mental illness very similar to that found in Simon's study. Jurors may ask themselves simply whether or not the defendant is so different from them that they cannot hold him responsible in the same way that they would hold themselves responsible. They look for bizarre acts, sudden episodes, a defendant's genuine obliviousness to his own best concerns, and a pervasive inability to lead an ordinary life—all things as convincingly conveyed by lay witnesses as by psychiatrists. They consider how reasonable the crime itself was: if the defendant murdered someone, whom did he kill, what motive did he have, and how likely does it seem that he might kill anyone else? If he stole, what did he take and what use did he have for it? They pay particular attention to evidence concerning his flight from the scene of the crime, any attempt to conceal his involvement, and his behavior upon arrest, all of which indicate a sense of rational purpose, a degree of sane planning, and an awareness of having done wrong.

The element that most influences jury deliberations and severely limits the number of insanity acquittals is the fact that, being randomly chosen from the population at large, jurors are as deeply suspicious of the insanity plea as is everyone else, and there is a commonsense notion of sane and insane, bad and mad, which transcends fashions in medical nosology and rests on a sense of everyday ethics. There are exceptional cases, where a jury will use the insanity defense as a "peg to hang its hat on" because they do not wish to convict a defendant they feel was not morally blameworthy when he technically broke the law. Otherwise, though, juries are very unlikely to acquit, no matter how peculiar the defendant may be. We try to believe that ours is an orderly world where one controls one's acts and takes credit or blame for them. An occasional defendant may be sufficiently bizarre yet sympathetic that juries set him beyond responsibility, but many "crazy" criminals seem so hideously strange and perverse that they are beyond the reach even of sympathy, and juries convict from a determination that such diabolical wickedness should never go free.

8

INCOMPETENCY
TO STAND TRIAL

There are two great fears about the insanity defense: that clever and wealthy defendants can feign insanity to elude justice, and that genuinely deranged maniacs, once acquitted, will be quickly turned loose on the streets. People have probably feigned insanity from time to time, though it is more difficult and rare than one might suppose. It is hard to find any definite cases, since most defendants who believe they have pretended to be mentally ill are mentally ill in fact. Moreover, a faked insanity plea would incur considerable risks, because if the defense fails, the defendant has sacrificed any chance he might have had to plea bargain, and has seriously compromised his efforts to contest the material facts of the case and therefore tends to receive a longer sentence. The only available comparative study on this point indicates that New Jersey defendants charged with robberies, assaults, or other serious offenses against persons, and who are found guilty despite a plea of insanity, receive sentences more than twice as long as similar defendants who do not plead insanity.[1] If, on the other hand, an insanity plea succeeds, the defendant will almost certainly be hospitalized and cannot be sure when he will be released.

Until very recently, an acquittal by reason of insanity was

only nominally different from a conviction. Though the law benevolently refrained from labeling a poor insane wretch "guilty," the powers that be made quite certain that this treacherously innocent person did not walk the streets. No statistics are available for the nineteenth century, but the defense then was most commonly raised against a murder charge: if convicted, the defendant was hanged; if acquitted by reason of insanity, he died more slowly in an asylum. Very few people acquitted of dangerous crimes because of their mental state were ever released from the secure wards of state hospitals and, had they been, one can feel confident that the insanity defense would not have survived the century.

This situation prevailed well into the 1960s. Institutional psychiatrists and the administrators of hospitals for the criminally insane tacitly accepted their role as jailers. These forensic facilities often fell under the jurisdiction of state correctional authorities rather than under mental health departments, and their operation was more closely oriented toward security than treatment: in fact, a 1963 American Bar Foundation research team inquiring about conditions at New York's Matteawan State Hospital was told that most of the inmates would have been far better off in a penitentiary. Many of the doctors were foreigners, often without psychiatric training or previous experience, and some did not speak enough English to carry on a worthwhile conversation. The staff were terrified of the patients and, rather than medicating violent cases, kept them constantly in straitjackets. Of therapy there was next to none, nor were there programs or recreational activities to help pass the years.[2]

Years was the very least NGRI inmates could expect to spend in institutions, and the hospitals' policy toward release was also more closely aligned to a correctional view than a medical one. One 1966 study showed that the superintendent and staff of Atascadero, California's maximum security psychiatric facility, had adopted unwritten guidelines such as the "ten year rule," whereby NGRIs originally charged with murder would not even be considered for release or transfer in less than a decade, regardless of their mental state.[3] An investigation of records at Pennsylvania's Farview State Hospital suggested "that a patient's mere presence at Farview constituted prima facie evidence that he should remain."[4] Forensic psychiatrist Dr. Ames Robey cynically remarks that a widespread old-time policy toward NGRIs entering a secure facility was that "whatever condition they showed at that point was their 'mental illness,' and if they showed nothing more than being a chronic undifferentiated DRC, then you were going to assume that that was the diagnosis that made them mentally ill. And you kept them until their DRCness had been cured, and then you'd let them go, which was usually when they were fifty, sixty, seventy years old. I assume you know what 'DRC' stands for. It's a complex technical term: Dirty Rotten Crook."[5]

One cannot discuss the disposition of persons found NGRI without also discussing the fate of those found incompetent to stand trial, an alternative route for the mentally ill offender which differs from an insanity verdict in interesting ways. Under our common law system of adversarial trials, the prosecution and defense battle for the verdict. The defendant has the advantage of a presumption of innocence which the prosecutor must refute beyond a reasonable doubt, and is guaranteed the right to know the charges against him, to examine the evidence, and to confront witnesses. Since the law is complex, the defendant is entitled to the assistance of counsel who will help him use the legal equipment devised for his benefit. As we will not tolerate a schoolyard bully's abuse of a smaller and weaker child, we do not consider it just to make someone fight in a courtroom, perhaps for his life, when he is incapable of defending himself. Yet some defendants, the severely mentally ill, may lack the ability to make rational use of their legal protections even when informed of the accusation, confronted with witnesses, shown the evidence, and aided by counsel, and these people are excused from the courtroom combat until they are well enough to defend themselves.

In early English law the distinction between incompetency and exculpatory insanity was less clear than it later became, and as the two concepts diverged, far more attention was paid to the criteria for an insanity acquittal, which was more dramatic and final, than to the supposedly temporary status of incompetency.

In the early-twentieth-century United States the criteria for competency to stand trial varied from state to state and from one court to another, and were nowhere much more precise than Blackstone's mid-eighteenth-century remark that if "the prisoner becomes mad, he shall not be tried; for how can he make his defence?"[6] In North Carolina, defendants "adjudged to be insane at the time of their arraignment . . . shall be sent by the court . . . to the hospital for the dangerous insane."[7] In Virginia, "[i]f, prior to the time for trial of any person charged with crime, either the court or attorney for the Commonwealth has reason to believe that such person is in such mental condition that his confinement in a hospital for the insane or a colony for the feebleminded is necessary for proper care and observation," the court could commit him. The court could, "in its discretion," appoint one or more medical specialists to examine the defendant, but this was not necessary.[8] In some states, such as Florida, there were no specific procedures at all, and the issue was left completely to the discretion of the trial judge, who, when upon "observation or suggestion" he might have reason to suspect insanity, was free to deal with the issue as seemed "best under the law."[9] What is surprising is not the ambiguity of the early statutes, but the fact that they did not change. New York's first statute concerning incompetency to stand trial was written in 1828, and though subsequent case law added some interpretation and refinement, the statute was not significantly revised until 1965.

In the twentieth century, the increased availability of psychiatric facilities and a growing tendency to regard antisocial behavior in psychological rather than moral terms meant that ever greater numbers of people were likely to be examined for competency, and to be examined for ever less flagrant reasons. An evaluation could be requested at any time between the moment of arrest and the end of the trial by the judge, prosecutor, defense counsel, or other interested parties. In many jurisdictions, certain types of offenses, such as murder, arson, or sex crimes, automatically lead to a psychiatric evaluation.

The ease with which a defendant could be subjected to a competency examination is indicated by guidelines described in 1964 by Dr. Charles Smith, then medical director of the United States Bureau of Prisons. The federal code permitted a competency evaluation upon "reasonable cause," which was interpreted to mean:

> whenever there is a history of mental illness or prior hospitalization; when there are unique and unusual circumstances, facts, or deviations surrounding the commission of the offense; or when there is some unusual or bizarre behavior observed while in detention awaiting trial or during appearance in court. Generally, it is also desirable to consider the mental competency of defendants charged with sex offenses, with offenses against persons such as assault, threatened assault, or the mailing of obscene or threatening letters. There have also been instances in which members of the defendant's family or friends have questioned his mental capacity because they were unable to understand or, perhaps, accept his criminal behavior.[10]

After casting the net so wide and examining defendants who showed such flimsy indications of abnormality, one might suppose that the majority of those evaluated would meet the rather modest requirements for competency, but Dr. Smith reports that of the first two hundred defendants examined, fully one-third were found incompetent to stand trial.

The number of people nationwide who were found incompetent was extraordinary. In the mid-sixties, more than ten times as many people were committed to mental institutions as incompetent to stand trial or for competency evaluations as were committed following an acquittal by reason of insanity.[11] At Matteawan State Hospital in 1962, 65 percent of those committed were there as incompetent to stand trial,[12] as were 74 percent of all patients there in 1968.[13] Of the 1,484 patients at Ionia State Hospital in Michigan during the month of August 1960, 47.5 percent were labeled incompetent.[14] In Massachusetts during 1964, 1,437 men, women, and children were sent by criminal courts to state mental institutions for pretrial psychiatric evaluation;[15] by 1967, the figure was 1,599—11 percent of the *total* admissions to the state's mental health facilities.[16]

There is nothing inherently wrong in such large numbers of incompetency commitments as long as there has been persuasive evidence that one is acting in the defendants' best interests by thus indefinitely suspending their constitutional right to a speedy trial, and as long as there are appropriate mechanisms for helping defendants regain competency and return to court to refute the charges against them. Unfortunately, the laws were quite vague on the legal nature and function of the incompetency finding, and judges and lawyers tended to turn the whole matter over to psychiatrists, who, without guidelines or qualifications, based their judgments on inappropriate medical models. This was forcefully brought to light in 1963 by a study of incompetency evaluations at Michigan's Ionia State Hospital. The "vast majority" of records showed that examining and testifying psychiatrists confused the standard for competency with the McNaughton test for criminal responsibility. In fact, much of the time they did not give much thought to any legal test at all, and most reports to the court did no more than copy the appropriate (or inappropriate) statute, inserting or omitting negatives as needed. *Not one* of the patients' records, psychiatric progress reports, staff conference notes, or discharge or parole certificates mentioned anything about legal standards of competency, speaking instead of "lacking in insight into his crime," "immaturity," "continues to be hostile," "uncooperative," "homosexual activity continues," or whether or not the patient was cheerful—all of which may have been diagnostically significant indices of mental state, but none of which addressed the question being asked, namely, whether the defendant could understand the charges against him and participate in his own defense.[18]

A slightly later study at a Massachusetts hospital[19] found psychiatrists making competency determinations exclusively on the basis of medical diagnosis: all psychotics were found incompetent, all nonpsychotics were found competent. Once again, all reports filed with the court were couched in Mc-Naughton terms. In other jurisdictions, examining psychiatrists confused incompetency criteria with the criteria for civil commitment, or with the presence of virtually *any* moderately serious, diagnosable mental ailment,[20] and it was clear that in some cases physicians were overstepping both their proper legal and medical roles to pass moral judgments. The competency report on one Ionia patient stated: "This man is a chronic alcoholic. He is impulsive and extremely dangerous. He is not treatable and should be sent to the hospital for segregation for a good long time, if not for life."[21]

If the procedures and criteria for entering a mental hospital because of incompetency to stand trial were so lax, it is hardly surprising that once patients got in, they were unlikely to get out. Competency is a relatively definable entity operationally related to the defendant's interests and role in court; normalcy is not, and if institutional psychiatrists waited for patients to be "cured" before returning them for trial, the defendants might have a long wait, particularly since most state hospitals

117

were overcrowded and understaffed, and serious reevaluations were correspondingly infrequent. It is significant that in a large proportion of cases where an attorney or the court expressed continuing interest in an incompetent defendant, the hospital reexamined him and found him competent. There is no reason to believe that these defendants were healthier than the rest; it was simply the case that unless someone asked, nobody ever looked at them again.

In 1901, a nineteen-year-old boy was accused of committing a burglary in Brooklyn, but was found incompetent to stand trial and sent to Matteawan. There were no periodic reviews of his condition, no regular reports to the court on any changes in his mental state, and sixty-four years later, at age eighty-three, he was still there.[22] It does not appear that the charges against him were ever dropped, conjuring the grotesque implication that if one day psychiatry certified him as cured, the district attorney would dig out his files, ghosts of dead witnesses would float into court, and this octogenarian would finally be tried and perhaps even punished for a dusty old crime.

In April 1905 a man was arrested in Flatbush for the theft of a horse, harness, and buggy.[23] He pleaded not guilty, but was found to suffer from "acute delusional insanity," declared incompetent to stand trial, and was also sent to Matteawan. Hospital records noted that he was sometimes violent during the early part of his stay, though in later years he was "docile and cooperative." His later years were indeed very late, since he was not released until 1964, when he was eighty-nine, following a motion to dismiss the original indictment.

Neither of these two men had been convicted of a crime, nor is there any reason to suppose that they would have been committed to a mental hospital had criminal charges never been filed. They carried their presumptions of innocence and a panoply of constitutional rights through most of the twentieth century, within the particularly unpleasant confines of a maximum-security hospital for the criminally insane, because the state was protecting them against the possibility of bungling their own defense and being wrongfully convicted. Yet they were not even charged with violent crimes, or ones that bore heavy sentences, and had they been convicted, whether rightly or wrongly, they would have been free before World War I.

These cases were extreme, but not unusual. A 1965 census of all 1,062 patients then being held at Matteawan as incompetent to stand trial[24] revealed that 208 had been there for twenty to sixty-four years, 252 for ten to twenty years, and 185 for five to ten years. Over 50 percent of the Ionia incompetents were expected to remain there for the rest of their lives,[25] and a study of incompetent patients in the state hospital at Bridgewater, Massachusetts, found that, before 1960, only a handful had been returned for trial at all, and that more people had left by death than through all other avenues combined.[26]

Prosecutors were not unaware of the results of an incompetency finding, and there is evidence that they sometimes took advantage of the flaws in the system "as a means of handling situations and solving problems for which there seemed to be no other recourse under the law."[27] Since the prosecutor could raise the issue of competency (because, as a servant of the state, he, too, wished to protect the defendant's rights), he could use it to dispose of people who had committed minor offenses with high nuisance value without going through the trouble of civil commitment proceedings.[28] It was possible to ensure the long-term sequestration of dangerous defendants without ever going to trial, even if the case against them was weak.[29] Sometimes when hospitals did try to return incompetents for trial years after their original commitment, it was found that the charges had been dropped. Ninety percent of the incompetent patients in Massachusetts hospitals in 1970 were found to have no charges pending: for over 40 percent, the charges had been dismissed on the very day that the accused had been committed, though neither he nor the hospital had been notified, strongly indicating that the prosecution considered its goal to have been accomplished.[30]

One of the most grotesque examples of the incompetency finding's abuse is the case of Albert Curt von Wolfersdorf, described in Bruce Ennis's *Prisoners of Psychiatry*.[31] In 1951, von Wolfersdorf and Joseph Paonessa were indicted on charges of murdering a thirteen-year-old boy in Poughkeepsie. The district attorney requested a sanity examination of von Wolfersdorf, and though the psychiatric report mentioned nothing about ability to understand charges, participate in his defense, or aid counsel, and gave remarkably little indication that there was any evidence of mental disease at all, the sixty-six-year-old defendant was found incompetent to stand trial and committed to Matteawan, safe from abuse at the hands of justice.

The most curious feature of von Wolfersdorf's case was that there was no evidence whatsoever against him except for the highly questionable testimony of his codefendant, Paonessa, a strange down-and-out fellow whom von Wolfersdorf had generously housed, clothed, and helped to find a job. Several months after the murder, Paonessa told the police that his friend had killed the boy, whose family rented an apartment in von Wolfersdorf's house. Later, Paonessa repeatedly changed his story, sometimes saying that von Wolfersdorf had done the killing, sometimes that he himself had done it, sometimes that he was present, sometimes that he was in one of several locations up to thirty-five miles away, or even that he had killed the boy but done so under von Wolfersdorf's "thought control." Paonessa was finally tried for the crime himself, convicted, and sentenced to death, and his execution in early 1953 obliterated every suggestion of von Wolfersdorf's implication.

Von Wolfersdorf, nonetheless, remained at Matteawan, protesting his innocence. He demanded a lie detector test; the district attorney would never reveal the results. On sixteen occasions he petitioned the court to find him competent so that he could stand trial and contest the charges against him. These were the only times during his stay at the hospital when staff psychiatrists interviewed him, and as they did not find him "improved," his petitions were denied. In 1969 he contacted Bruce Ennis, a lawyer then with the New York Civil Liberties Union, and they filed a succession of unsuccessful writs of habeas corpus in state courts.

In 1970 von Wolfersdorf's case was heard in a federal district court; by this time he was not even requesting release, but merely, after almost two decades, at age eighty-six, a transfer to the less onerous surroundings of a civil hospital. An assistant attorney general battling to keep the defendant at Matteawan was obliged to concede that there was "no speck of evidence on which relator could be tried," and yet, as the presiding judge remarked in his decision, he had been "locked away in a place more likely to drive men mad than to cure the 'insane.' "[32]

The court held that von Wolfersdorf's confinement violated his Eighth and Fourteenth Amendment rights to due process and protection against cruel and unusual punishment, and ordered him transferred out of Matteawan. Within a month of his arrival at a civil facility in Binghamton, hospital authorities said there was no need for continuing treatment and that they were prepared to release him as soon as suitable arrangements had been made for his relocation in the community. His release was not possible, however, while criminal charges were still pending, and Ennis had to return to the district attorney with a request for dismissal. Finally, in January 1972, the D.A.'s office consented and a court motion was made, but for obscure reasons the judge refused to dismiss and ordered the district attorney to prosecute.

The case ended at last on December 4, 1972, when von Wolfersdorf entered a courtroom to face a twenty-two-year-old murder charge. The assistant district attorney immediately petitioned the court for a psychiatric examination to determine the defendant's competency. The judge would not grant it. At that point, the prosecutor admitted that there was no evidence whatsoever against von Wolfersdorf. Said Ennis, "I think they were embarrassed to tears to admit it and wanted him to live out the rest of his life in the hospital."[33] The case was closed, and soon afterward von Wolfersdorf was released from the hospital, a free man at age eighty-eight.

The situation of NGRIs was similar to but even worse than that of the more numerous and more fully studied incompetents, for a variety of reasons. Whereas the population of those given competency evaluations included defendants accused of all sorts of crimes, those people acquitted by reason of insanity had most often been accused of crimes against persons, dangerous acts, and other serious felonies. Moreover, whereas the incompetent defendant who left the hospital was turned over to the criminal justice system for trial and ultimate disposition, in the case of the NGRI, the hospital psychiatrists carried the unpleasant burden of knowing that their diagnostic opinion was all that stood between the patient and complete freedom. Even if the patient had behaved himself well amid the controlled routine of the hospital, there was no telling what he might do when left on his own and plunged into the uncertainties of the outside world. Neither doctors nor administrators cared to have one of their NGRI alumni appear on the front page of newspapers under the headline RELEASED MANIAC MURDERS SIX. Thus, barring conspicuous sanity and innocuousness, or pressure and some sort of supervisory guarantees from concerned family and friends, there was little incentive for mental hospitals to release NGRIs, and they did not.

Everyone closely involved with the system knew well what the fate of an NGRI would be. This is one reason why so many insanity defenses succeeded or passed uncontested by the prosecution. Everyone had the warm inner satisfaction that he had done the right thing for this poor mentally ill individual, had spared him the terrible stigma of a criminal conviction, kept him out of the dreadful prison, and had arranged to have him looked after by medical specialists. Everyone also knew that he would probably never see this defendant free again, and that an insanity acquittal was a very safe sort of mercy to extend.

9

THE REVOLVING
DOOR

This situation changed dramatically and fairly abruptly due to the confluence of a number of factors. The development of psychoactive medications, beginning in the 1950s, made possible the outpatient treatment of many previously untreatable cases. In the sixties and early seventies attention was drawn to the atrocious conditions and lack of treatment in many of the state mental hospitals, which were serving as little more than warehouses for people who often did not need to be there and who had been committed according to the most casual, sometimes unscrupulous, procedures. A sequence of court decisions made clear that involuntary hospitalization was, in fact, a complete deprivation of the individual's liberty, similar to imprisonment, and that society should not lock someone away simply because it was thought to be in that person's best interests. Deprivation of liberty could be justified only if the person was a danger to himself or to others and thus gave society a right to take emergency steps. He must be given the benefit of a hearing and representation by counsel to contest the allegation that he was in need of involuntary confinement. Once confined, he was entitled to treatment aimed at his rehabilitation and release, and he had the right to periodic court reviews of his status, so that his confinement would not endure beyond the time when he was either cured or no longer dangerous.

Corresponding changes took place in the realm of the criminally committed patient. The first of several major cases in this area was *Baxstrom* v. *Herold*,[1] decided by the Supreme Court in 1966. Johnnie Baxstrom was convicted in New York of second-degree murder in 1959 and given a two-and-a-half- to three-year sentence. In June 1961 a prison psychiatrist certified him insane, and he was transferred to Dannemora State Hospital, a secure mental facility under Department of Corrections jurisdiction that accepted mentally ill convicts from the prison population. In December of that year, Baxstrom's prison sentence expired, and though in the state psychiatrists' opinion he was still mentally ill, he no longer fell under correctional authority. Efforts were made to transfer him elsewhere, but the Department of Mental Hygiene refused to accept him in a civil hospital. He finally remained at Dannemora, though officially under Mental Hygiene jurisdiction. Baxstrom's subsequent petitions for either release or transfer to a civil facility were unsuccessful, and he was still at Dannemora in 1966 when his appeal reached the U.S. Supreme Court.

The Supreme Court held that Baxstrom had been denied equal protection because he had never been given the type of hearing, proper representation, and jury review which the laws of New York offered to other civilly committed patients. The mere fact that he had previously been at Dannemora while serving a prison term in no way furnished acceptable and sufficient proof that he was presently in need of involuntary care in a secure facility. In response to the director of Dannemora's contention that the state was justified in treating people such as Baxstrom differently because their criminal convictions had proven them dangerous and hence in a different category from the civil insane, the court stated:

Classification of mentally ill persons as either insane or dangerously insane of course may be a reasonable distinction for purposes of determining the type of custodial or medical care to be given, but it has no relevance whatever in the context of the opportunity to show whether a person is mentally ill *at all.* For purposes of granting judicial review before a jury of the question of whether a person is mentally ill and in need of institutionalization, there is no conceivable basis for distinguishing the commitment of a person who is nearing the end of a penal term from all other civil commitments.[2]

The *Baxstrom* decision had far-reaching results for two reasons. On the one hand, since the Supreme Court decision had invalidated a New York procedure by which mentally ill prisoners could be detained in a hospital at the expiration of their sentences, all cases previously disposed of in this way had to be reexamined, and under what came to be called Operation Baxstrom, nearly one thousand patients were transferred from Dannemora and Matteawan to civil hospitals. There was outraged protest from employees of civil hospitals who feared this inundation of the criminally insane, and from residents who lived near these hospitals and worried about having dangerous maniacs in the neighborhood. Their grim expectations were not met. Four years later, less than 3 percent of these supposedly dangerously insane people had been returned to correctional facilities or hospitals for the criminally insane, while fully 27 percent were living peaceably unsupervised in the community,[3] leading to a recognition that the institutional psychiatrists were greatly overestimating these patients' potential for violent behavior, and were keeping them under close restraint for far longer than could be legally justified.

It became evident that the issue could not be limited to the peculiar situation of the *Baxstrom* patients—a group of convicted prisoners maintained in mental health facilities without having been properly committed—but that once one questioned the validity of procedures for committing the insane in the criminal system, one could not stop after the first arbitrary foray. The *Baxstrom* case dissolved a long-standing reluctance on the part of criminally committed patients to seek their release through the courts, and a reluctance on the part of the courts to hear the few cases that arose. Previously there had been a tacit acceptance of the premise that NGRIs were a unique category, outside the regular rules of the law, but this belief was now thrown into question in a flurry of court cases.

In 1968 the principles first raised in *Baxstrom* were specifically applied to the insanity defense. Gerald Bolton, who had been acquitted by reason of insanity two years earlier on charges of stealing a car, and automatically committed to St. Elizabeths Hospital under existing District of Columbia statutes, filed a writ of habeas corpus challenging his automatic commitment. He claimed that though he had been insane at the time of the theft in 1965, by the time of his trial the following year he had undergone psychiatric treatment and was no longer mentally ill in a way that would warrant involuntary hospitalization.

The D.C. Circuit Court of Appeals agreed that there were conspicuous flaws in the procedure.[4] Under Washington law at the time, once the defendant had raised the issue of insanity, the prosecutor had to refute it—as he had to prove all other elements of the charge—beyond a reasonable doubt. Thus an insanity acquittal signified only that there was a reasonable doubt that the defendant was sane at the time of the crime, and was certainly not an affirmative determination that he was insane and committable at the time of his trial. The court also noted that there were great differences between the statutory provisions for an NGRI commitment and a civil commitment; the latter required judicial determination of insanity and periodic hospital review of mental state, whereas an NGRI commitment required neither and simply relegated the patient to psychiatric limbo. The court held that, in keeping with *Baxstrom,* there was no justification for this distinction. The only permissible difference in treatment ought to be that an NGRI could be automatically committed for a limited evaluation period, since the fact of his criminal behavior and his insanity at the time of the crime gave tangible reason to suspect present mental illness and dangerousness, though it in no way proved it.

The area of incompetency to stand trial was undergoing similar change. A 1960 Supreme Court decision, *Dusky* v. *United States,*[5] defined the factors to be considered in an incompetency hearing in terms of the defendant's ability to participate in the legal process, and laid solid grounds for appeals of any future improper findings. This, combined with the alarming studies of incompetency abuses, spurred tremendous interest in the field. The first systematic outline of incompetency examination procedures was published in 1965,[6] and within a very short time its author was inundated with reprint requests. By the end of the sixties, there was a sizable literature on competency, and psychiatrists, lawyers, and judges were all much more familiar with the issues to be considered. Since incompetency determinations were now tied to the appropriate questions of capacity to understand the charges, ability to assist counsel, and sufficient mental stability to withstand the rigors of a criminal trial, the numbers of people found incompetent were reduced.

Attention was also turned to the question of how long someone found incompetent to stand trial could remain hospitalized. In large part as a result of the *Baxstrom* decision, a few states instituted procedural changes. In 1969 the Supreme Judicial Court of Massachusetts decided[7] that a commitment while awaiting trial was a *civil* commitment and that, in consequence, the defendant must be afforded all of the procedural protections given in noncriminal involuntary proceedings, including periodic review and evaluation for release according to the strict new standards governing competency. As a result, the number of prolonged incompetency commitments in that state was halved in one year.[8] In 1971, New York State enacted legislation requiring the release of defendants charged with misdemeanors after ninety days, and dismissal of charges against felony offenders when their commitment had lasted for two-thirds of the maximum possible prison sentence for the crime charged against them.[9] The situation was changed for the rest of the country by the 1972 Supreme Court decision in *Jackson* v. *Indiana*.[10]

Theon Jackson was a twenty-seven-year-old mentally defective deaf-mute. His tested mental age was that of a preschool child, and he had only a limited use of sign language. In May 1968 he was charged in Marion County, Indiana, on two counts of robbery stemming from two incidents the previous year in which he had allegedly stolen money and property worth a total value of nine dollars. A competency evaluation was requested, and two psychiatrists testified at the hearing. Both doctors said that Jackson's mental deficiency combined with his minimal communication skills rendered him unable to understand the charges against him or effectively to participate in his defense: one deemed it unlikely that Jackson could ever achieve any proficiency in sign language, and the other stated that, even were he not a deaf-mute, he would probably not be competent to stand trial. The prognosis, as one put it, "appears rather dim."[11] Not surprisingly, Jackson was declared incompetent and placed in a state mental hospital, there to remain until, according to statute, he "shall become sane."

The case was not that unusual, except for its extremity, since, given the dim prognosis for recovery, it appeared quite evident that Theon Jackson would spend the rest of his life hospitalized because of an unproven nine-dollar theft. Jackson's court-appointed attorney was furious, and appealed the case to the top Indiana court twice before finally reaching the U.S. Supreme Court.

The Supreme Court held Jackson's commitment to be in violation of his equal protection and due process rights. In *Baxstrom* it had decided that conviction and sentencing were not sufficient reason for depriving a person of the procedural and substantive protections guaranteed to others, from which it followed that "the mere filing of criminal charges surely cannot suffice."[12] The trial record, however, nowhere showed that Jackson met civil commitment criteria, and the testifying psychiatrists had never examined him for this purpose. The state's contention that Jackson's present detention was only temporary rather than indefinite did not impress the justices: the record offered no hope that he would improve, and the state hospital could do nothing to help him improve, so that his internment there served no therapeutic purpose. Furthermore, had he been civilly committed, his present condition would probably merit release, since except for the unproven charges against him, he had always been able to get by under home care and was even employed at times. He was not dangerous to himself or to others, nor incapable of taking care of his own basic needs. Under an incompetency commitment, however, he would be ineligible for release unless there was a substantial improvement in his condition, which there clearly never would be.

> We hold, consequently, that a person charged by a State with a criminal offense who is committed solely on account of his incapacity to proceed to trial cannot be held more than the reasonable period of time necessary to determine whether there is a substantial probability that he will attain that capacity in the foreseeable future. If it is determined that this is not the case, then the State must either institute the customary civil commitment proceeding that would be

required to commit indefinitely any other citizen, or release the defendant. Furthermore, even if it is determined that the defendant probably soon will be able to stand trial, his continued commitment must be justified by progress toward that goal.[13]

The Supreme Court declined to address directly the question of whether or not charges should be dismissed if it was shown that an incompetent would never regain competency, but mention of "the denial of due process inherent in holding pending criminal charges indefinitely over the head of one who will never have a chance to prove his innocence"[14] made the Court's sentiments fairly clear: if a defendant can never defend himself, he should never be tried.

Theon Jackson's case was remanded to the original trial court, where he was found incompetent and unlikely to regain competency in the foreseeable future. The judge dismissed the charges. Under civil procedures he was not committable, and after three and a half years in the hospital, he went free.

The conglomerate of these decisions, from *Baxstrom* to *Jackson*, left matters in a very awkward state. Fewer people were being found incompetent, and those who were spent less time hospitalized as such. Some of them could be civilly committed, though this, too, was becoming an increasingly difficult procedure. Others were being sent on to trial, where they might or might not raise an insanity defense. Those who did succeed in pleading insanity, however, were no longer automatically banished to the eternal purgatory of hospitals for the criminally insane, because the law had backed itself into a corner and, following the implications of its own rules to their logical, somewhat irrational result, maintained that when an insanity acquittal came in, the crime disappeared and the defendant was cleansed of all taint. The *Jackson* decision seemed such a loud and clear mandate that criminal and civil cases should be treated equally that some jurisdictions went so far as to abandon automatic commitments even for purposes of examination, leaving it entirely to the court to institute civil commitment proceedings. The newly acquitted NGRI, it seemed, suspected only moments before of hacking his wife into little bits and setting her out with the trash, was theoretically in the same legal position as any other citizen who chanced to be in the courtroom at the time, and there was no more reason to detain one than the other.

It was only natural that some disasters should occur once the age-old status quo was upset. Defendants whom prosecutors had let plead insanity as a means for getting them out of the way were now getting out. Some newly acquitted offenders, to the surprise of the courts and the district attorneys, were not going in. In some jurisdictions, whole hospital populations had to be reexamined in accordance with the new rules. It is particularly interesting to observe what took place in Michigan, which encountered massive problems and, to solve them, devised not a new insanity test, but a novel form of insanity verdict: Guilty But Mentally Ill.

10

GUILTY BUT
MENTALLY ILL

In Michigan in March 1970 James Chester McQuillan was charged with attempted rape. He was acquitted by reason of insanity and automatically committed to Ionia State Hospital until such time as he should be found sane and no longer a danger to society. The twenty-two-year-old McQuillan, a high school dropout who had served in Vietnam until the previous August, when he had been diagnosed as a paranoid schizophrenic and discharged from the army with a 100 percent psychiatric disability, did not think he should remain hospitalized indefinitely. He denied any recollection of the attempted rape, and in an interview with a *Detroit Free Press* reporter admitted that he needed help in dealing with his violent impulses but said that state and prison hospitals did not provide the sort of social rehabilitation he thought that he ought to have.[1]

After spending about a year at Ionia, McQuillan filed his own petition with the Wayne County Circuit Court, stating that his indefinite confinement without periodic examination and review violated his rights under the state constitution and the Sixth and Fourteenth amendments to the U.S. Constitution. The court agreed, and appointed a psychiatrist to examine McQuillan. The doctor found him to have some "personality problems," but no mental illness sufficient to merit his continued confinement in a mental hospital,[2] and as a result, McQuillan was released on December 22, 1972.

The state of Michigan appealed the Wayne County court's 1972 decision to vacate McQuillan's automatic commitment, and in September 1974 the state supreme court finally handed down its decision in *People* v. *McQuillan*,[3] upholding the lower court ruling.° Drawing heavily on recent U.S. Supreme Court decisions such as *Baxstrom*, the court declared that Michigan's automatic commitment procedures did indeed violate state and federal requirements of due process and equal protection and were "constitutionally repugnant,"[4] since a finding of NGRI proved only that the People had failed to make their case for conviction against the defendant, but did not, and were not intended to, reach a conclusion on his committability. It was therefore ordered, as in *Bolton* v. *Harris*, that NGRIs could be held automatically only for a limited period of examination and observation, and must otherwise have the same rights, protections, and release provisions as the civilly committed.

In addition, *McQuillan* stated that anyone who had already been held under the existing Michigan statutes for more than sixty days without examination and observation must be examined within sixty days of the decision's date, and then either be notified for a hearing within ten days, or discharged. There were at the time an estimated 270 NGRIs held by Michigan hospitals, meaning that the state's centralized Center for Forensic Psychiatry at Ypsilanti had only two months to examine and report upon 270 people, and court commitment proceedings had to be held for any of them deemed unfit for release. Says Dr. Ames Robey, then director of the Forensic

° At the time of the *McQuillan* decision, McQuillan himself was in a Topeka mental hospital. He had gone to Kansas the day after his release from Ionia, but was arrested two months later on burglary charges. Following his conviction and imprisonment he was diagnosed as schizophrenic and transferred to the state hospital.

Center, "I found out later that the court figured there might be ten or twelve to review, and they thought they were being *very* generous. They had *no* idea of the statistics."[5]

Robey himself had been compiling statistics on NGRIs for a number of years, and had noticed a disturbing trend: in fiscal year 1967–68 there had been 12 insanity acquittals in Michigan; during the two-year period from 1968 to 1970 there were 15; in each of the subsequent three years there were, respectively, 37, 51, and 54. He predicted that by 1977–78 there would be over a hundred, and that the number would continue to rise.[6]

Of even greater concern were the results of a 1973 study concluding that of all NGRI commitments in Michigan since 1967, 53.4 percent were not legally and medically appropriate.[7] A year later, Robey conducted a more thorough study of the 350 NGRIs then in the system[8] and found that only about 20 percent appeared to have a serious mental illness that was causally related to the crime. Another 50 percent displayed varying degrees of neurosis or psychosis, but by the standards Robey set at the Forensic Center they should not have been found exculpable. The remaining 30 percent were not mentally ill at all, nor did it appear that they ever had been.

Previously, this large group of "inappropriate NGRIs," having strayed into a mental hospital, would have been kept there by psychiatrists and administrators in the interest of protecting society. Following the *McQuillan* decision, this odd form of psychiatric vigilantism was no longer possible. Reviews were required, and a patient could easily take his case to court, represented by counsel and aided by his own psychiatric witnesses. He might be exceedingly dangerous, but if he did not meet the simultaneous criteria of being dangerous *and* mentally ill, he had to be released. Following the Forensic Center's hasty post-*McQuillan* review, approximately 150 NGRIs were discharged from Michigan hospitals in late 1974.

One person released under the *McQuillan* decision was

Ronald Manley, who in January 1974 had been acquitted by reason of insanity of a 1972 rape charge. Psychiatric testimony at his post-*McQuillan* committability hearing was mixed, but the court ultimately decided that he did not meet the standard for continued involuntary hospitalization. On March 22, 1975, ten weeks after his release from the Forensic Center, Manley forced a pregnant woman and her five-year-old son into a vacant garage with an ice pick. He bound and abandoned the child, then took the woman to three other locations where he repeatedly raped her before she managed to escape. Soon afterwards, Manley and another man raped, robbed, and beat another woman.[9] Manley was arrested three days later, and the following year he was convicted on two counts of rape, two of armed robbery, kidnapping, sodomy, and assault with intent to rape.[10]

Another *McQuillan* case was that of John Bernard McGee. In December 1973 McGee shot a drug addict in the back, killing him. The following June he was found not guilty of the crime by reason of insanity and sent to the Forensic Center. McGee had been implicated in a number of other crimes, and after handing down the verdict, the judge offered McGee immunity if he would help clear up these unsolved cases. McGee confessed to twelve murders, and his detailed accounts of the killings convinced police that he was, indeed, responsible for at least seven of them. McGee later told a psychiatrist that he had really killed twenty or twenty-five people. Sometimes he killed for hire, charging, he said, anywhere from a thousand to fifteen hundred dollars, but other killings had been done for revenge or out of anger. It was reported that some of McGee's friends had once gotten together to discuss plans for killing him: it was "not because they hated McGee or even disliked him, but because he had killed too many of their friends for no good reason and nobody knew who might be next. 'We saw it as an obligation to the neighborhood,' " one of them said.[11]

Following the *McQuillan* decision, McGee's commitment came up for review, and the state went to court to keep him hospitalized. There was evidence of his previous crimes; one security supervisor from the hospital testified that McGee had threatened to have him killed.[12] Nonetheless, the six-person jury did not feel that the state's presentation met the civil commitment requirements. "Oh, Christ," Forensic Center director Ames Robey was quoted as saying,[13] "I can't think of many people that we've had here that are apparently more dangerous than he is, but who am I to argue with the wisdom of a jury?" The majority of the jurors told reporters that they believed McGee was indeed dangerous, but faulted the prosecutor for calling a single psychiatrist to testify, and said that it had not been adequately proved that McGee's dangerousness was the result of mental disease. One of them predicted, "I bet this guy goes out and kills somebody within a month."[14] The prosecutor said that the jury had done its work to the best of its ability, stating, "I assign complete judicial misconduct to our Supreme Court for its inept and incompetent [*McQuillan*] decision."[15]

The one pessimistic juror was right: on April 15, 1975, John McGee beat and stomped his wife to death. When his case came to trial the following year, McGee refused to attempt an insanity defense, saying that he did not believe he was insane and did not want to submit to the mental health system again. He pleaded guilty to first-degree murder, which in Michigan carried a life sentence with no possibility of parole. McGee's own mother, who testified at the trial, was quoted as saying, "He ain't nothing but a killer."[16]

The people of Michigan were understandably incensed. By June 1975, four NGRIs discharged from state hospitals had committed serious crimes, and the newspapers gave them front-page coverage. Part of the blame, admittedly, could be attributed to the undue haste with which the authorities were forced to rush through hundreds of cases, and part from the

problems encountered during any transition from old laws to
new, but no one could guarantee that the same thing would
not happen again.

Ames Robey had been trying to find a solution to the
problem of inappropriate NGRI commitments for some time,
and in the months before *McQuillan* was handed down, when
legal barometers indicated that some such decision was in the
air, he hit upon a novel proposal. The main problem, Robey
believed, were the 50 percent of NGRI forensic patients who
his recent study indicated were neurotic or psychotic but not
in a manner causally related to their crime. The verdict
appeared to him to be the result either of the jury's misun-
derstanding of the distinctions in the insanity rule, or of a
mistaken belief that an insanity acquittal was the best way to
guarantee that the defendant would receive treatment within
a secure facility. The proper disposition would have been to
convict them, since they were responsible for the crime, and
then to give them psychiatric help within the prison system.

Under Robey's proposal, the insanity defense was left intact
and unchanged, but a new verdict, Guilty But Mentally Ill
(GBMI), was insinuated between the verdicts of guilty and
NGRI. If the defendant lacked "substantial capacity either to
appreciate the wrongfulness of his conduct or to conform his
conduct to the requirements of law," he would be acquitted
by reason of insanity as before. If he was proved guilty and
was not mentally ill, he would, of course, be convicted. But to
help the jury find its way through the complex area between
those extremes, jurors were offered the alternative of finding
a defendant GBMI if he was shown to satisfy three criteria:

    a) that the defendant is guilty of an offense

    b) that the defendant was mentally ill at the time of that
offense

    c) that the defendant was not legally insane at the time
of the commission of that offense.[17]

Since there was no causal relationship between the illness and the crime, a verdict of GBMI was a conviction and carried the same sentence as any other conviction for the same crime. The only difference the new system would make for the GBMI defendant himself was that he would, it was claimed, arrive at the prison with a sort of GBMI flag attached that would alert the prison authorities that here was someone in need of treatment, and someone whose psychiatric state should perhaps be taken into account during parole hearings.

The interesting thing about the Guilty But Mentally Ill legislation, which Michigan adopted in 1975 and has used ever since, is the difference between what it promised to do and what people hoped it would do. Robey claimed that there was confusion in applying the insanity test, and that GBMI would reduce the number of insanity acquittals by fine-tuning the distinction and eliminating those who would not fall under the existing rule if it were properly applied. But it is quite obvious that the greatest appeal of the GBMI legislation was to people who did not care about such niceties, and simply thought that there were too many insanity acquittals altogether, and that GBMI was a way to get rid of them. Robey himself admits that even in Michigan, following the *McQuillan* decision and the results of his study on Forensic Center NGRIs, "the immediate impulse of the legislature was to abolish the insanity defense,"[18] and this idea was dropped only when it was pointed out that, in light of the abortive Washington and Mississippi attempts, it was unlikely that such a move could survive a constitutional challenge.

The circumstances surrounding the adoption of GBMI in other states make it quite clear that the hope everywhere was to reduce insanity acquittals. Indiana was the first state to follow Michigan. In 1977, Indianapolis real estate developer Anthony Kiritsis was found NGRI after holding a loan company executive hostage with a shotgun wired to his neck and parading him before news cameras. In 1978, California Angels baseball player Lyman Bostock was shotgunned to death in Gary when he strayed across the line of fire of a man trying to kill his own wife. The killer was subsequently acquitted by reason of insanity and released after spending six months in the hospital. As a result of public outrage over these crimes, the legislature proposed a GBMI bill, which became law in 1980.

Illinois followed in 1981. When Governor James Thompson had first suggested that the state either abolish the plea of insanity or adopt a "guilty but insane" or "guilty but mentally ill" verdict, it was amidst the uproar over the case of Thomas Vanda.[19] Vanda had been charged with stabbing a fifteen-year-old girl to death on the street in November 1971. After committing the crime he telephoned the police, waited beside the body, and made a full confession. Many psychiatrists who examined him agreed that he was legally insane, and when he finally went to trial in June 1975 he was acquitted by reason of insanity. The Director of the Illinois Department of Mental Health later said, however, that as soon as Vanda was committed following his acquittal, he showed no further signs of insanity. "There were times when the people at Madden [Mental Health Center] felt 'There is nothing wrong with this guy.' We had him for about 10 months, and he never showed any sign of psychosis that we could see. Behavior like that does raise one's eyebrows. In the period of nearly a year, we should have seen something."[20] Nonetheless, Vanda did not appear to be mentally ill and committable, and was released.

Within a year, Vanda had stabbed a woman to death. A psychiatric report filed with the court in July 1977 stated that he was competent to stand trial but legally insane at the time of the crime. At about the same time Vanda sent a one-page letter entitled "How to Beat a Murder Rap By Insanity" to another man then awaiting trial for murder, who turned the letter over to the state attorney's office. The letter suggested such tactics as telling doctors "you are hearing voices and . . .

those voices told you to do your crime," breaking out in
hysterical laughter, claiming that Rorschach ink blots look like
two men having sex with each other, and masturbating in front
of the staff members.[21] Psychiatrists were quick to say that
such amateur ruses would not fool them and that insanity was
nearly impossible to fake during a prolonged observation
period, but in light of Vanda's history, the public was not
so sure. In a matter of months, the legislature introduced a
GBMI bill.

The remaining six states which had instituted GBMI by
early 1983—several of them, too, after abortive abolition
attempts—all passed the legislation in the wake of the John
Hinckley trial: four of them in June 1982, the very month
when Hinckley was acquitted by reason of insanity. At least a
dozen more states and the federal government began considering similar bills. It seemed clear that the public and the
proponents of GBMI believed that mistakes had been made in
the cases of Ronald Manley, John McGee, Anthony Kiritsis,
Thomas Vanda, John Hinckley, and many others. As a Harvard
law professor who supported a "guilty but insane" verdict
wrote in the *New York Times*:[22]

> John W. Hinckley, Jr. is not obviously insane. It took
> considerable expertise to convince attentive jurors of his
> insanity. A friend who attended the trial said to me, "If you
> had been there, you would understand how crazy this guy
> is." But to many of those who were not there and who,
> therefore, were not swept along by the testimony of the
> psychiatric experts, Mr. Hinckley seems like a kid who had
> a rough life and who lacked the moral fiber to deal with it.

The insanity defense was permitting juries to make mistakes,
and GBMI was seen as a way to stop them and to send these
dangerous borderline defendants to jail.

Many people were under the impression that the insanity
defense was to be completely eliminated by the GBMI legis-

lation and that henceforth all insane criminals would fall under correctional authority, being treated in a mental hospital until they were well, and then transferred to the penitentiary to serve out the remainder of their term. Others, who knew that the insanity defense was still there alongside GBMI, nonetheless supposed that the new verdict would expand to envelop all mentally ill defendants, and thus abolish the insanity defense for all practical purposes by forcing it into desuetude. One could claim that the addition of another verdict would enhance judges' and jurors' ability to perceive the distinctions between the fact of mental illness and the fact of criminal responsibility, and help them properly to apply the law, but as critics and advocates alike often confessed, it was far more likely that a jury faced with a difficult case would take the easy way out and opt for the seeming compromise verdict of GBMI. After a token acknowledgment that the defendant was sick, poor fellow, they would remember just how dangerous he had shown himself to be, and select the verdict that would put him away.

Fortunately or unfortunately, these hopes were not realized. It is a rather sorry coincidence that in 1982, when so many states were seeking to solve their problems by following Michigan's lead toward GBMI, Michigan itself was reviewing seven years' worth of experience with the legislation and coming to the realization that it did not seem to work as intended or as hoped. For that matter, it did not seem to do anything at all.

Whatever it was expected that juries might think, GBMI is not, of course, a compromise verdict, but a conviction. In accordance with the statute, to reach that verdict a jury must ascertain that the defendant was guilty and was not legally insane, just as they would for anyone else who unsuccessfully raised the insanity defense. Since the criteria for legal insanity had not changed, the division between those who were culpable and those who were exculpable should have remained precisely the same—the psychiatric examination results would still sort defendants out according to whether or not they satisfied the ALI test, and additional information on mental illness short of legal insanity would serve only to distinguish defendants who were guilty and apparently mentally sound from defendants found to be guilty but mentally ill.

Judges and juries appear to recognize this more clearly than legislators supposed. In a recent study, researchers from the University of Michigan Law School compared the numbers and types of people found NGRI before 1975 with the total populations of people found NGRI and GBMI after 1975.[23] Had GBMI worked as most had assumed, recent years would show few or no insanity acquittals, and one would find a new population of GBMI defendants approximately equal in number to those who had previously been found NGRI. Jurors would have been tricked by the appearance of compromise, and coerced by their fear of a dangerous madman's early release into entering GBMI verdicts regardless of expert testimony.

This did not happen. Between 1972 and 1975, 0.025 percent of all adult males arrested in Michigan were found NGRI. In the years since, 0.026 percent have been found NGRI. In absolute numbers, this means that an average of fifty to sixty defendants are acquitted by reason of insanity in Michigan each year: they were before GBMI took effect, and they have been since. In the years since 1975, however, this number has been supplemented by an annual average of thirty-four defendants found GBMI. Though it is impossible to say with certainty what would have become of these defendants had GBMI not been available as an alternative verdict, a thorough examination of various demographic characteristics, the types of crimes committed, previous arrest and hospitalization records, and current psychiatric diagnoses, indicates that those defendants found GBMI more closely resembled convicted criminals than NGRIs, and led the researchers to the conclusion that "at least a majority of the GBMI defendants would have been found guilty in the absence of the GBMI statute."[24]

According to the best evidence, then, what the GBMI statute was doing was not imprisoning mentally ill defendants who would previously have been acquitted, but simply adding the label "but mentally ill" to the guilty verdict of defendants who would have been convicted anyway. This could have been a useful rather than merely confusing distinction if the classification made some difference in the treatment of the GBMI convict, but this, too, appeared not to be true. What, after all, had been done? Merely that the jury had decided that the defendant, who was guilty, was also mentally ill—clearly a preposterous thing for the jury to do. If, as had been maintained throughout the *Durham* experiment, it was not the psychiatrist's role to determine social questions of guilt and responsibility, one can certainly find no justification for asking a lay jury to make a legally irrelevant, purely medical, diagnosis of whether or not the defendant was mentally ill. Moreover, such a determination could have no useful effect on the convict's subsequent institutionalization.

Wayne State University law professor Ralph Slovenko has repeatedly stated that if a jury correctly understands and applies the law, " 'guilty but mentally ill' is just another way of saying 'guilty,' "[25] and that "but mentally ill" carries little more meaning than any other extraneous remark that might be jotted in the margin of the prisoner's dossier. If one cares to say "guilty but mentally ill," one might just as well institute verdicts of "guilty but flat feet," "guilty but appendicitis," "guilty but a headache," "guilty but long fingernails," and then once the jury has made these irrelevant amateur medical diagnoses, when the convict arrives at the prison he will be given corrective shoes, surgery, two aspirin, or a manicure.

In fact, well before the GBMI legislation was passed, Michigan statutes required psychological testing for all convicts in correctional facilities and appropriate care for those who needed it, and many states have held that there is a constitutional requirement to furnish treatment for mentally ill prisoners. Dr. John Prelesnik, superintendent of the Reception and Guidance Center at Jackson State Penitentiary, sees everyone who enters the Michigan prison system, and says that GBMI has not altered anything.[26] Of about two hundred GBMI convicts he had received by 1982, about half were mentally ill, and of them only twenty-five were considered in need of treatment. The remainder either had not been mentally ill in the first place, they were ill in a way that did not indicate special treatment, or they had been ill at the time of the crime (which is all the GBMI verdict claimed), but after perhaps years of hospitalization for incompetency and pretrial therapy, and after the simple passage of time between indictment and conviction, they had recovered or gone into remission and were no longer in need of treatment. Moreover, his routine psychological screening identified the mentally disturbed among the new arrivals without the impertinent and rather pointless assistance of the GBMI verdict. His screening, in fact, indicated that approximately 15 percent of the regular convicts who enter the prison system without having pleaded insanity or being adjudicated GBMI were mentally ill and in need of treatment, meaning that the GBMIs were not very different from everyone else, but, unfortunately, the prison psychiatric facilities were inadequate for any of them—a crucial point which the GBMI legislation never addressed.

In Michigan, then, the Guilty But Mentally Ill legislation, though it has created some confusion and triggered a continuing legal controversy, has had no noticeable effect on the fate of defendants contesting their guilt by reason of insanity. Whether or not the original assumption was true that there were NGRIs who seemed medically inappropriate when they reached the forensic hospital, the failure of GBMI to reduce the number of acquittals seems to indicate that judges and juries have always adequately distinguished between mental illness that

11

ABOLISHING
THE DEFENSE

Guilty But Mentally Ill sought to limit the number of insanity acquittals by leaving the terms of the test unchanged while insinuating an additional verdict onto the jury ballot that would resemble a compromise while having the effect of a conviction. In the wake of the John Hinckley trial there was a flurry of efforts, particularly at the federal level, to reverse the trend of the past hundred years and reduce the number of acquittals by tightening the basic criteria for insanity. A prominent psychiatrist suggested that the ALI rule might be made more restrictive by changing the word "substantial" to "severe," and inserting the word "entirely," thus requiring for acquittal that a defendant, "as a result of *severe* mental disease or defect," lack *"entirely* the capacity to appreciate" the wrongfulness or criminality of his conduct.[1] One Senate bill quite simply proposed casting the ALI rule aside and going back to McNaughton.[2]* The greatest amount of attention,

---

* The change that was ultimately made combined these two suggestions. The "Insanity Defense Reform Act of 1984," signed into law on October 12, 1984, placed the burden on the defense to prove that "the defendant, as a result of *severe* mental disease or defect, was unable to appreciate *the nature and quality or the wrongfulness of his acts.*" The precise wording of the verdict was also altered to read "not guilty *only* by reason of insanity."

however, was lavished on a handful of bills proposing a seemingly radical solution: the complete abolition of the separate insanity defense.

The abortive attempts by two states early in the century to ban psychiatric testimony from criminal trials made it quite clear that the issue of insanity cannot be divorced from the question of guilt without raising serious constitutional objections. One could, after all, conceive of degrees of mental illness so acute that a defendant's behavior would seem like the mindless activity of an automaton, and he could not possibly entertain the intent elements required for conviction of his crime. In at least these extreme cases, to prohibit evidence of the defendant's glaring abnormality would be to deprive him of his right to contest all elements of the charges against him.

The new abolition efforts aimed to skirt the constitutional objections very neatly and precisely by admitting psychiatric testimony, but *only* in those cases where it addresses questions of intent. All special tests, such as McNaughton or ALI, would be abandoned in favor of the simple statement that it shall be a defense "that the defendant, as a result of mental disease or defect, lacked the state of mind required as an element of the offense charged. Mental disease or defect does not otherwise constitute a defense." The separate, blanket defense of insanity would be abolished, and a mentally disturbed defendant could bring in psychiatric witnesses only to litigate the *mens rea* or intent elements of crimes, which require, for example, that an act have been done "knowingly," "negligently," or "with intent to" do something. This form of abolition is consequently also called the *mens rea* test, and its advocates believe that it will be much more restrictive, and will largely eliminate the battle of psychiatric experts by limiting their testimony to very narrow questions of what the defendant meant to do, without delving into the secret psychological machinery that led to the act.

The first jurisdiction to abolish its separate insanity defense was the state of Montana,° which did so quietly and almost unnoticed in 1979, well before the Hinckley trial sent legislatures everywhere scurrying in search of solutions to the perceived menace of insanity acquittals. According to Judge Michael Keedy, a former Montana state representative who introduced the abolition bill, the legislature's reasoning was simply that the insanity defense gave mental illness a status in the criminal justice system that it did not properly deserve, and introduced vague and often meaningless psychological discussions into what was essentially a social and moral issue. Legislators felt that Montana's ALI test, relying on critical terms such as "appreciate" and "conform," tended to draw attention to areas that had nothing to do with culpability, nor even, necessarily, with mental illness. There are lawbreakers who do not "appreciate the criminality" of their conduct because they feel some inner justification for what they have done, but "the Montana legislature didn't believe that a defendant's own impressions of himself, or his personalized view of his conduct, should have a thing to do with society's judgment; and so it rejected that aspect of the insanity defense based upon one's ability to 'appreciate the criminality' of his conduct."[3] The control arm of the ALI test, which stated that a defendant was not guilty if he was "unable to conform his conduct to the requirements of law," appeared similarly inappropriate, since this could pertain not only to the deranged defendant whose illness annihilated his capacity for self-control, but appeared to be "an apt description of a *chronic criminal*— the very defendant we most want incarcerated and removed from society."[4]

Opponents of the Montana bill complained that one ought not to convict a defendant who did not know what he was doing, to which the reply was that no one *would* convict a

° Idaho passed similar legislation in 1982.

defendant who was *truly* oblivious of his actions. Such a person would lack the necessary *mens rea,* and since a guilty intent is an element of a crime, without that intent there would be no crime, and the defendant would be acquitted, and would then, if appropriate, be subject only to ordinary civil commitment procedures. These cases were expected to be quite rare, however, since in Keedy's view, "today, in Montana, a defendant ought to be able successfully to invoke an 'insanity defense' only if the jury entertains a reasonable doubt that, because of a mental disease or defect, he was able to act *knowingly* or *purposely.* [Montana's criminal code defines 'knowingly' as being aware of one's conduct, and of the high probability of what the results are likely to be; it defines 'purposely' as a conscious object to engage in certain conduct or to cause a particular result.] The test is thus so narrow, and a finding of 'not guilty by reason of insanity' is now such an improbable expectation thereunder, that I do believe Montana has successfully eliminated insanity as a defense."[5]

In later post-Hinckley discussions of proposals for a federal *mens rea* test, advocates were more strident and specific about the anticipated results. As Attorney General William French Smith stated to the Senate Judiciary Committee in July 1982, under a *mens rea* formulation,

> mental disease or defect would be no defense if the defendant knew he was shooting at a human being to kill him—even if the defendant acted out of an irrational or insane belief. Mental disease or defect would constitute a defense only if the defendant did not even know he had a gun in his hand or thought, for example, that he was shooting at a tree. This would abolish the insanity defense to the maximum extent permitted under the Constitution and would make mental illness a factor to be considered at the time of sentencing, just like any other mitigating factor. It would eliminate entirely as a test whether a defendant knew his actions were

morally wrong and whether he could control his behavior. It would also, of course, eliminate entirely the presentation at trial of confusing psychiatric testimony on this issue.[6]

An associate attorney general addressing the same Senate committee surmised that a bank robber seeking an insanity acquittal under the *mens rea* test would need to present psychiatric testimony, not that he had delusions, heard voices, or was subject to overbearing compulsions, but that he thought "he was in Egypt and not in the bank," or that he had "the equivalent mental age of a 2- or 3-year-old."[7] These situations, he rightly believed, would be extremely infrequent, and when they did arise, the defendant's mental condition would be so conspicuous and acute that the expert testimony would be clear, indisputable, and all but unnecessary. "Psychiatrists don't, as often, disagree over someone having a mental age of 2 or 3, as they are prone to be able to disagree over people operating from irresistible impulses or some of these vaguer concepts."[8]

This view of the relationship between mental illness and crime, if it prevailed, would return the insanity defense to a very early, strictly cognitive view of legal insanity according to which a defendant could be convicted if he knew and intended his actions, however insane the perceptions, motives, and compulsions behind that knowledge and intent might be. It is a concept of exculpatory mental illness dating from James Hadfield's day, when the prosecutor attempted to prove sanity, reason, and hence responsibility by reminding the court that the defendant was bright enough to stand on his seat, where he could get off a clear shot above the heads of the other spectators. Under such a law, John Hinckley would clearly have been convicted. George Remus and Harry K. Thaw would have been convicted, and Ronald Manley and John McGee. So, too, would have been Arnold, Ferrers, Hadfield, Bellingham, Oxford, McNaughton, and Roderick Maclean. Those few defendants who might properly merit acquittal would be those who only just barely contrived to be competent—who were able to understand the charges against them even though they were unaware of what they had done. In Attorney General Smith's analogy, they would be people who did not know that they were holding a gun, did not know what guns were for or how they operated, did not know they were shooting at a person, and yet somehow, miraculously, shot someone.

Psychiatrists have been quite alarmed by the potential of a *mens rea* insanity defense. Dr. Randolph Read has expressed fears that if testimony on delusion is prohibited and evidence restricted to the defendant's superficial knowledge and purpose, it might no longer be possible to distinguish legally between the case of a drug dealer who correctly felt persecuted by federal agents and who killed a suspected informer to protect himself and his livelihood, and the case of a psychotic housewife who killed while under the paranoid delusion that she was being persecuted by a conspiracy of Israeli secret agents and Mexican mafiosi.[9] Others suggest that an exculpatory disorder would have to be so severe that it produces a complete mistake of fact, as in an often cited hypothetical case where a man strangles his wife to death thinking that he is squeezing a lemon.* But as psychiatrist Jonas Rappeport indignantly told a Senate committee, "I have, in my 25 years of experience, never evaluated anyone who thought they were squeezing a lemon instead of a human being. That is superficial, simplistic, and a totally inaccurate view of mental illness."[10]

The abolitionists' hope and the psychiatrists' fear that insanity acquittals will all but vanish under a *mens rea* test, however, is based on the assumption that once the separate insanity defense is abolished, everything else will remain the same,

---

* This hypothetical example first appeared in the commentaries of the American Law Institute's Model Penal Code, and has enjoyed great popularity in discussions for the thirty years since, though the object of the defendant's murderous assault has sometimes been given as an orange, grapefruit, melon, or cabbage.

and courts will continue to interpret and apply *mens rea* concepts just as they always have done. This seems very unlikely. Existing definitions of intent elements are relatively vague and intuitive, and contain an implicit, though very tentative, assumption that the defendant is a normal person who recognizes and intends the natural and probable consequences of his acts. Intent is related to subjective attitudes of the defendant, but under ordinary circumstances it is discussed in terms of objective evidence and the inferences that jurors can make from that evidence based upon their general understanding of human nature. Even when the issue under consideration is an entirely internal emotional event, such as a state of passion produced in the defendant by some act of provocation, which could reduce the degree of homicide from murder to voluntary manslaughter, the jury is invited to understand the defendant's response not in terms of the nuances of his unique personality, but according to whether or not a hypothetical reasonable man would similarly have lost control of himself under the same provocation. Some jurisdictions allow the doctrine of "diminished capacity," whereby abnormal mental states can reduce the degree of a crime, but psychiatric evidence there has generally been limited to instances of intoxication, coercion, organic disorders, and other specific and rare conditions. Whenever there was question of a form of mental disorder so extreme and pervasive that it obliterated the defendant's capacity to understand the law, to appreciate the import of his own behavior, or to govern his actions, the matter has not been litigated in terms of *mens rea,* but has been shunted into the separate insanity defense.

This is, in fact, precisely why *mens rea* has been able to remain a comparatively tidy and neglected subject, and to avoid such troublesome problems as distinguishing between sane intent and insane intent, or between the awareness and consciousness of an ordinary man and that of a manic-depressive psychotic. *Mens rea* provided the logical and constitutional justification for the existence of an acquittal due to severe mental illness, but *mens rea* terms did not need to accommodate the unusual psychological concepts raised in connection with this issue, because a separate insanity defense was right there, phrased in terms which—however inadequate, outdated, or wrong they were—had been created for the specific purpose of determining mental responsibility. Without a separate insanity defense, the burden of sorting through these murky issues may fall on intent terms which are incapable of handling them.

There appears to be something inherently perverse about the insanity defense, which, as its history shows, never responds to legislative change in the manner legislatures anticipate. A hint that the *mens rea* test would be no exception can be found by glancing at the variety of people who have supported it at one time or another, and the contradictory purposes for which they have done so. The earliest recommendation to abolish the separate insanity defense and to rely completely on *mens rea* was made in 1915 by a committee of the American Institute of Criminal Law and Criminology.[11] Far from being an attempt to limit the role of psychiatry in criminal trials, the proposed model legislation, as Justice Doe's New Hampshire Rule, was intended to free psychiatric witnesses from the bothersome and archaic restraints of legal insanity tests, and to permit them to describe mental illness in all its forms, degrees, and symptoms, using their own terms, giving juries the benefit of current scientific knowledge. The chairman of the committee was confident not only that every type of evidence admissible under the McNaughton Rule would be admissible under a *mens rea* test, but that the new formulation would permit previously excluded evidence on irresistible impulse and other noncognitive disorders.[12] The committee even anticipated that the model legislation would permit evidence on diminished capacity, a doctrine not at all widely accepted at the time.[13]

154

Half a century later, an influential article by Joseph Goldstein and Jay Katz entitled "Abolish 'The Insanity Defense'—Why Not?"[14] suggested that since *mens rea* was already part of the criminal law, a separate insanity defense was at best superfluous and at worst a sinister fiction designed to permit the indeterminate confinement of defendants who, because insane, might lack the requisite *mens rea* and therefore be properly entitled to a full and unqualified acquittal and freedom. The authors suggested that the insanity defense really only concealed the extent of the law's confusion on the subjects of mental illness and dangerousness, and that one might best begin to clarify the issues of who should be held responsible and whether and why they should be restrained by abolishing the insanity defense and seeing what happened. Though they did not predict how this would work out in practice, they believed that the existing definitions of *mens rea* terms were so garbled and inadequate that such an experiment would inevitably lead to a major reexamination of the law's philosophical assumptions about such concepts as free will and blame.

In the early 1970s, the Nixon administration unsuccessfully attempted to pass *mens rea* legislation in Senate bills S.1400 and S.1. These proposals, part of Nixon's effort to "bring America back" from the permissiveness of the sixties and to restore "peace in our land,"[15] were aimed at the virtual elimination of the insanity defense, which the President felt had been the subject of "unconscionable abuse," and inexplicably singled out for particularly vehement attack. Both bills were widely criticized by psychiatrists for what was seen to be a barbarically narrow concept of mental illness. The proposal eventually died, dragged down with the rest of a hotly debated criminal code reform bill.

Paradoxically, these abolition efforts were favored by Judge David Bazelon, whose views on the ideal criminal justice system were often diametrically opposed to those of the Nixon administration. This issue was no exception, since he believed that the *mens rea* test had potential consequences drastically different from those desired by the drafters of S.1400 and S.1.

> . . . unlike some abolitionists who see abolition as a way of avoiding any inquiry into responsibility, I see abolition as a way of broadening the inquiry beyond the medical model. Admittedly, our concept of *mens rea* is as primitive now as our insanity concepts were over 20 years ago. But once freed from the "insanity" label as framed by the medical model, *mens rea* offers the opportunity and hope of proving more hospitable to a broad inquiry into all forms of disabilities and motivations.[16]

In other words, according to Judge Bazelon's radical view, the very act of deemphasizing an insanity defense based on psychiatric disorders might open criminal trials to the consideration of educational, cultural, and economic disadvantages as contributing factors to criminal behavior which, just as legal insanity, could reduce the degree of a charge or excuse a defendant from guilt.

The force of tradition, if nothing else, would probably serve to keep the *mens rea* test from expanding as far as Judge Bazelon might wish, yet it would quite probably also prevent it from dwindling into the vestigial remains of an insanity defense that the Nixon and Reagan administrations have hoped for.

One of the great presumed advantages of the *mens rea* test is that it will do away with confusing psychiatric testimony and eliminate the battle of the expert witnesses. It is a complete mystery, however, why this should happen. Disagreement among expert witnesses is peculiar, not to psychiatry, but to our criminal justice system. Forensics experts testifying on fibers and bloodstains, structural engineers seeking to assign blame for a fatal accident, and ordinary physicians disputing the degree of a victim's disability routinely disagree, and, just as with psychiatrists, the expert opinion of each tends to buttress the claims of the side that has called him. As long as experts are allowed into court, they will disagree.

It is claimed that without a separate insanity defense, psychiatric evidence will at least be more specific in its thrust and less radical in its possible effect on the verdict. The charge of burglary, for example, requires breaking and entering with the intent to commit a felony, and abolitionists suggest that under a *mens rea* formulation, psychiatric evidence could be limited to this single, simple intent question: did he or did he not intend to commit a felony? Moreover, even if, due to mental disease or defect, the defendant lacked this requisite intent, he might still be convicted of breaking and entering, which does not require such an intent, and he would be kept (and presumably treated) within the criminal justice system. But again, this assumes that even in the absence of a separate insanity defense structure to accommodate psychiatric evidence, courts would continue to apply a very narrow definition of intent elements. Would a court really refuse to hear evidence to the effect that, due to mental disease or defect, the defendant thought that the building was his own house and that he had to break in because he had forgotten his keys, or that he believed the structure was filled with poison gas and an infant was suffocating inside, or even that it was the hideout of Martian spies and that the ghost of J. Edgar Hoover had deputized him to gather information for the FBI? When mental illness is involved, one cannot neatly circumscribe the question of intent.

U.S. Senator Howell Heflin has voiced fears that the *mens rea* test could greatly *increase* the amount of psychiatric testimony. As an example,[17] he cited a congressional bill making it illegal to disclose the identities of CIA agents, an offense for which the prosecution is required to establish beyond a reasonable doubt a number of state of mind elements, among them that the defendant intended to identify and expose covert agents, that he had reason to believe that such exposure would impair the activities of the American foreign intelligence service, that he knew that the United States was trying to conceal the identities of such agents, and that he knew his disclosures did, in fact, identify those agents. For a normal person, one could reasonably infer these assorted mental states from the acts without logically proving them to a mathematical certainty. With a separate insanity defense, one could dispose of any contentions of exculpatory mental disease or defect as an independent, global issue. But in the absence of a separate defense, if it was contended that the entire illegal scheme was the product of an insane delusion, one could well be obligated to explore the meaning of each mental element of the charge within the context of that delusion.

Former Yale Law School dean Abraham Goldstein has expressed a comparable fear and suggested that the *mens rea* test is potentially very similar to the *Durham* rule, and susceptible to the same fate. Juries would be cast adrift amidst amorphous questions about the relationship between mental illness and responsibility. The field would open up to a profusion of litigation on the meanings of intent terms, and in the end, the courts would be forced to make "evidence of mental disease so freely admissible that it would call into question some of [the] objective notions of criminal liability that [are] bed-rock for the way in which we administer our concept of mens rea."[18]

Another scholar observes that even under the most conservative interpretation, the *mens rea* test could not conceivably be made more restrictive than the McNaughton Rule, since

[a] total inability to know the nature and quality of the act quite plainly precludes convicting a defendant of any crime whose definition requires that he have that knowledge. And any crime which requires intent or knowledge or recklessness, surely posits that knowing. If it were not for the special,

pre-emptive defence of legal insanity, therefore, the defendant would have a complete defence on the merits to any crime—namely, the lack of *mens rea*.[19]

Once one has gone so far as to admit the McNaughton type of testimony, though, one would expect the *mens rea* test then to follow the same evolution that McNaughton did. Even in the nineteenth century, most courts conceded that a man who was able to say, "Yes, I know that I killed him, and I know that it was wrong, and therefore I will apologize the next time I see him," was not really aware of the enormity of his crime, and the mere ability to recognize pistols and victims and to utter some superficial acknowledgment of what he had done did not prove him to be the sort of maliciously purposive murderer we choose to punish. Courts and legislators were reluctant to liberalize the verbal formulation of the insanity defense, yet long before the ALI rule actually introduced the word "appreciate" into the formula, usage had come to demand that a defendant have some more profound comprehension of his behavior than mere cognitive awareness that it was wrong. One can scarcely imagine that modern courts would resort to a more antiquated conceptual dictionary when interpreting the law.

As mentioned in an earlier section, judges under McNaughton were loath to prohibit any psychiatric testimony with some claim of relevance to the issues at hand, and were even accused of erring in the opposite direction and allowing far more of such evidence than was technically obligatorily admissible. This is natural and humane. It is also legally wise, since to exclude evidence that might affect the defendant's guilt could constitute reversible error, and the peculiar nature of psychiatric testimony makes its relevance difficult to ascertain until it has been heard. The *mens rea* test could make judges even less likely to bar psychiatric evidence, since under that form of rule pathological states of mind would no longer be a separate consideration. The defendant's psychological capacity to form the requisite intent would be an intrinsic facet of the charge that the prosecution must prove, and if a judge prohibited defense evidence on lack of control or lack of awareness with respect to a state of mind element, he would be directly preventing the defendant from contesting the charges against him.°

Perhaps the best demonstration of the changes that can be forced on definitions of intent is found in the disastrous history of California's experiment with the bifurcated trial. What began as an effort to limit the proliferation of psychiatric testimony and to clarify the issues for the benefit of the jury ended up nearly doubling the quantity of psychiatric evidence, creating what has been called a "junior insanity defense"[22] under which, during the guilt phase of the trial, the jury was

---

° The *mens rea* test could bring about several other procedural changes, such as requiring the prosecution to assume the burden of proving sanity, and mandating the doctrine of diminished capacity. The Supreme Court has held that, within the context of a separate insanity defense, it is permissible to place the burden of proving insanity upon the defense, because the prosecution still has the much heavier burden of proving all other elements of the charge, including intent, beyond a reasonable doubt.[20] With the *mens rea* test, however, the defendant's sanity becomes part of intent, hence an element of the charge itself, and the prosecution must assume the burden of proving it beyond a reasonable doubt.[21] To do otherwise would violate the defendant's presumption of innocence. At present only about half of the states place the burden on the prosecution, and though in most insanity trials either the evidence is sufficiently persuasive or the jury's conclusion is sufficiently independent of such legal niceties that the placement of burden is not of decisive significance, in close cases it could make a difference. A frequent criticism of the Hinckley trial was that the defendant might not have been acquitted but for the fact that the District of Columbia's law forced the prosecution to prove his sanity beyond a reasonable doubt.

The states are also about equally divided on allowing psychiatric testimony to reduce rather than to negate a charge. The legal justification for prohibiting such evidence is vague, but appears to rest on the assumption that as long as there is a separate insanity defense to deal with the global issue of mental abnormality, the defendant's rights are protected, and the court need not subdivide insanity. Once the law specifically stipulates that evidence demonstrating a relationship between mental disease or defect and the intent elements of a crime shall be admissible, however, it should be impossible to limit such testimony *only* to cases where the mental disease was alleged to negate *all* of the mental elements.

160

invited to evaluate not only the defendant's intent, but the *quality* of that intent and its relationship to the intent of other people. Rather than cutting down on confusion, bifurcation gave defendants two shots at essentially the same thing under slightly different names. "You can change the name of the game," one critic of the *mens rea* test remarked,[23] "but you cannot avoid playing it so long as *mens rea* is required." California's difficulties might well arise more quickly and acutely under a full *mens rea* test, where there would be no second trial to console those who might worry about the wrongful conviction of an insane person during the first, guilt-phase proceeding.

Such practical problems have not yet surfaced in the two states that have abolished their separate insanity defenses, though neither has a particularly heavy criminal case load. In Montana, there has been a slight decline in attempts to raise insanity at trial, though according to Assistant Attorney General Marc Racicot, who assists county prosecutors statewide in the preparation of major felony cases, there were very few attempts even before Montana adopted the *mens rea* test in 1979, and the insanity defense had never been perceived as a significant problem in their criminal justice system. Moreover, he is not at all confident that this decline is anything more than temporary: "the passage of the new law has created a certain amount of trepidation on the part of defense counsel and the mental health profession. They think that the defense is gone. I'm not sure that it is. But they think that it is, and in my view, that has probably had more impact on the decline in such pleas than anything."[24] Both Racicot and former representative Michael Keedy, the original sponsor of the legislation, concede that once defense counsel and expert witnesses gain sophistication in dealing with the new law, *mens rea* may well have the potential to turn back into a regular insanity defense.[25]

Meanwhile, one problem that has begun to surface in Montana courts is that of terminology. The Attorney General's office initially opposed the *mens rea* bill for the very reason that, though juries were familiar with such concepts as "conforming" and "appreciating criminality," and a workable set of rules and procedures had evolved over the years, there were no guidelines at all for the new type of law. Indeed, for the first several years insanity trials were plagued with faulty instructions: judges attempting to explain what kinds of mental disease or defect negated intent, and what "negating intent" actually meant in the first place, told jurors that it would be, for example, a type of mental disease that made the defendant unable to appreciate the criminality of his conduct or to control it.[26] Within the context of *mens rea*, judges simply could not think of a good way to describe the concept of legal insanity, nor, apparently, did they fully understand the new law themselves: "I wish somebody would explain it to me," one district judge was quoted as saying.[27] After a time, there was an attempt to develop new jury instructions, but it is not clear how successful this effort has been,[28] since, though they have eliminated the inappropriate ALI language, they have not replaced it with anything useful to lay jurors, but merely reiterated the rule that for a defendant to be acquitted by reason of insanity, his mental disease or defect must preclude the requisite state of mind, whatever that means. There has yet to be a major contested case that challenges the hypothesis that all relevant medical testimony can be channeled into the purely legal *mens rea* terms.[29]

University of Virginia law professor Richard Bonnie mentions a homicide case in which the defendant's mental state, though it presented a fairly coherent pathological picture, could be handled only with great difficulty in terms of a strict *mens rea* application. Joy Baker, a thirty-one-year-old Virginia woman, admitted that she had shot her aunt to death.

Her testimony, which was not doubted by anyone who ever heard it, was that she thought her aunt had been possessed

162

by the devil and that [her aunt] and all the other people in the community were part of some demonic conspiracy to annihilate her. She felt that she was immediately threatened at the time that her aunt suddenly appeared at her back porch. . . .

Joy Baker shot her aunt two times. At the time of the first shot, she believed that her aunt was possessed. However, when she shot her aunt, and her aunt fell backwards into the mud on the back porch of the house, she realized at that time in a more realistic way what she had done. Her aunt said, "Why, Joy?" "Because you are the devil and you came to hurt me," Joy answered. Her aunt said, "Honey, no, I came here to help you." At this point, the defendant said she saw that her aunt was hurting and became very confused. Then, according to her statement, she said, "I took the gun and I shot her again just to relieve the pain she was having because she said she was hurt." Her aunt died after the second shot.[30]

The arresting officers and residents of the community believed that Baker must be insane. Every psychiatrist who examined her said that she was acutely psychotic and out of touch with reality at the time of the crime. Under a traditional insanity defense such as Virginia's McNaughton Rule, she would undoubtedly have qualified for acquittal, since she did not appreciate the nature and quality of her act, nor, arguably, even understand that it was wrong. According to Professor Bonnie's analysis, however, if Baker were tried under a *mens rea* rule, she would properly have to be convicted following a tortuous debate not merely over her state of mind, but her states of mind at the time of each of the two shots.

At the time of the first shot, Baker believed that she was killing, not a human, but the devil, and that she was doing so in self-defense. Yet this was an unreasonable mistake of fact— i.e., not one that a reasonable person would make—supplying only an imperfect justification for the deed, and she would, according to ordinary procedures, be convicted of at least some lesser crime, such as manslaughter or negligent homicide.[31] For the second shot, however, Professor Bonnie concludes that a different situation existed:

> At the time of the second shot, Ms. Baker was in somewhat better contact with reality. At a very superficial level she "knew" that she was shooting her aunt and did so for the non-delusional purpose of relieving her aunt's pain. But euthanasia is no justification for homicide. Thus, if we look only at her legally relevant "state of mind" at the time of the second shot, and we do not take into account her highly regressed and disorganized emotional condition, she is technically guilty of murder.[32]

Clearly, however, no jury would view Joy Baker as a fit subject for punishment and convict her of murder and, if her mental state made her not responsible for murder, it would seem unjust to resort to the sham compromise of convicting her on a lesser charge. As it happened, when Joy Baker's case came up in reality, even under a McNaughton Rule, the court, with the consent of the prosecution, merely dismissed the charges after a preliminary hearing, and there was never even an indictment.

If the law is made unduly harsh, one can expect to see more cases where the law is simply not invoked in the first place. Alternatively, courts and attorneys will develop new procedural methods to achieve what is seen as a just result in spite of the law, whether by dismissing charges, negotiating pleas, or, as has already been happening in Montana, by simply agreeing, without contest, that due to mental illness, the defendant lacked the requisite intent and was therefore legally insane.

It is interesting to note in this context that most of the *mens rea* proposals, while ostensibly tightening the criteria for an insanity acquittal, partly counter this firm attitude by granting the sentencing judge an extraordinary range of dispositional options for dealing with a defendant who is convicted despite a serious mental illness. The most striking instance of this discretionary power is found in Montana's 1979 law, which would never have weathered opposition in the legislature without such special provisions. If a judge determines in the sentencing hearing, based on the psychiatric evidence presented during the trial as well as any other evidence he deems useful, that a defendant who failed in his insanity defense "was suffering from a mental disease or defect which rendered him unable to appreciate the criminality of his conduct or to conform his conduct to the requirements of law," he can waive any mandatory minimum sentence.[33] Thus, conceivably, a jury that had wrestled with the difficult question of the relationship between insanity and intent and rejected the defendant's plea in accordance with a strict *mens rea* test, could then see the presiding judge invoke the outlawed ALI rule to reduce greatly or even to eliminate completely a sentence that the law would have mandated for any other defendant.

The various *mens rea* sentencing provisions do, of course, also make various stipulations about mental health care and prison-to-hospital transfers, but these are more administrative than substantial, since no jurisdiction that has adequate psychiatric facilities to offer would deny treatment to *any* convict who needed it, whether he had attempted an insanity defense or not. The only practical justification for giving the judge exceptional powers in disposing of an unsuccessful NGRI lies in a fear that the insanity test may have been made so strict that it might demand the conviction of some whom we do not wish to punish. At worst, this is akin to a court's wiping out annoying cases where legal protections cause the acquittal of culpable people by adopting policies that would convict everyone, and then letting the innocent benefit from the judge's discretion or work their way out on appeal. At best, such a system pretends to solve the problems of the insanity defense

12

THE QUESTION
OF DISPOSITION

Ultimately the *mens rea* formula may be the most reasonable and logical form of insanity test, since it removes the ancient illusion that there is a neat, all-or-nothing distinction between "them" and "us," and between the mad and the bad. It could open the field to a long overdue discussion of what we in modern times truly mean by intent and responsibility, of how far we are willing and able to go in viewing each criminal defendant as a unique individual who is only partially in control of his own personality, and of what purpose a criminal justice system should now be expected to serve. Initially, however, and for a long time to come, *mens rea* would simply translate the words of the ALI rule and recent versions of McNaughton into a new formulation that will work just the same way.

Mentally ill defendants, after all, are not acquitted because of the insanity defense or because of modern psychiatric theories. The insanity defense exists in the first place because basic human sentiments and a social concept of justice that far predates psychiatry have caused the law to be as it is. The past century's trends in legislative, judicial, psychiatric, and social attitudes indicate that there is a point beyond which one simply cannot limit the insanity defense, because it expresses a strong, if imprecise, opinion about where we draw the line between those whom we consider responsible members of society and those for whom we, as a humane and enlightened society, ought to feel responsible. The various insanity "tests" are merely our best attempts to articulate a succinct, official statement of who those people are whom we want to excuse, and studies of jurors' comprehension of insanity tests and judges' instructions indicate that the moral judgment involved in an insanity acquittal is largely independent of precise wording. One can reasonably suppose that it would consequently resist strictly verbal alterations in the law.

Undoubtedly there are mistaken verdicts from time to time, and there always will be, whether it is in the insanity defense or in another area. Witnesses lie, evidence is distorted or suppressed, investigators make mistakes, one lawyer does a better job than the other. Above all, the fundamental legal tenet that it is better to acquit ten guilty defendants than wrongfully to convict one innocent man makes it statistically certain that we will err. But though laws may take on a life of their own and diverge from the intention that spawned them, rarely, if ever, does the letter of the law demand and receive an insanity acquittal that is contrary to society's common sense of justice, and though critics often claim that the insanity defense is readily abused, there are very few clear cases that support this contention.

In the majority of the relatively few successful insanity cases, even the prosecutor has agreed that the defendant is insane and does not contest the plea. Very often the offender's illness so obviously precludes legal responsibility that he never even reaches a courtroom—charges are simply dismissed, either outright or in exchange for guarantees of voluntary or involuntary civil commitment. One might surmise that if there is pressure to limit the insanity defense beyond a certain commonly accepted point, more cases would be informally rerouted as the authorities found other, less visible, ways to avoid sending insane people to prison. At present, it is extremely difficult to compile accurate statistics on the disposition of NGRIs; if these defendants were dispersed through a multitude of other channels under a variety of other names, they would still exist, but it would become impossible even to identify them.

Given the apparent inevitability of insanity acquittals, the important and troublesome question is really not which test we use, but what we do with the defendants when they leave the courtroom. Centuries ago, when the law was less intricately developed, more was left to common sense and the exigencies of the moment, but as we sought to arrive at more equitable, generally applicable rules, we sacrificed some of this flexibility. In 1800, alarmed at the possibility of James Hadfield's release, Britain rushed through legislation authorizing the immediate indefinite hospitalization of a defendant whose very acquittal was presumed to offer incontrovertible proof of his dangerous lunacy. Similar procedures were adopted in America, and for a century and a half afterward no one needed to worry about insanity acquittals of any kind, since NGRIs were left quietly to languish and die in psychiatric warehouses alongside their civilly committed brethren.

It is quite clear, however, that many mental disorders can go into remission or vanish altogether, particularly with the help of modern therapies. A person so acutely deranged as to lack moral awareness or control at the time of his crime may recover after years in a hospital or even in the interval before his trial, and it could only be a sinister form of disguised punishment to retain such a person in a mental hospital for longer than his clinical condition warranted.

In the 1960s the courts recognized the abuses that resulted from making psychiatric commitments too easy and appeals against them too remote from the grasp of hospitalized patients and, in response, seemed to lean to the opposite extreme and assume that the *parens patriae* power of the state would always be misused unless rigorously challenged and questioned at every step. Strict new criteria for involuntary civil commitment were laid down permitting the detention of the sick for only so long as their inability to cope with freedom outweighed their right to possess it: to be deprived of his liberty a person must be an immediate danger to himself or to others. A sequence of court rulings further stated or implied that NGRIs, having been acquitted of all crime, were no longer criminal defendants, were outside the reach of the court, and, except for a brief postacquittal examination period, could not be committed under less stringent procedures than those applied to civil patients nor made to meet more stringent requirements for release. They had become a medical rather than a criminal concern.

As a statement of philosophical principle, this concept is laudable, but as a rigid procedural guideline it invites problems. Every city in the country has encountered difficulties with the new civil commitment standards, whose medically and socially naive requirement of a narrowly defined present dangerousness to self or to others leaves thousands in an unacceptable state of misery: they are ineligible and inappropriate for total hospitalization, but unable to cope on their own, yet there is no intermediate level of aid available.

A patient is released, or can successfully demand his release, if he has not been shown to be recently dangerous. He has, however, usually been in a closed hospital environment where he may have spent several years among familiar surroundings with a regular schedule, under medical supervision, on medication, without drugs or alcohol, away from family- and work-related stress. One is asked to accept this as sufficient proof that he will function competently and safely when he is abruptly turned out into a totally unsupervised world and told to accept full responsibility for himself, to find a job and some self-respect, to resist the temptation of drugs and alcohol, and to reintegrate himself among family and friends who have learned to get by without him and who may be the very people he hurt most before his hospitalization. Hospitals have no authority to mandate continuing medication or psychotherapy, or to make release contingent upon attendance at aftercare programs. Such facilities are generally available on a voluntary basis, but typically those patients whose condition deteriorates most are the ones least likely to continue taking their medicine or to make wise decisions about seeking psychiatric help. In consequence, recent years have seen a pattern among certain mental patients of release, relapse, and finally rehospitalization when their state has deteriorated enough to satisfy involuntary commitment requirements.

This situation can be especially worrisome not only to the patient but to the community around him when the person is an insanity acquittee. It is quite obviously nonsense to suppose that there is no difference between an NGRI and a civilly committed patient. They may be mentally ill in ways that are, somehow, pathologically similar, but in one case the illness has manifested itself in a criminal act, quite possibly a violent one, while in the other it has not, and patients who are violent under certain conditions are likely to be violent when those conditions recur. Nonetheless, most courts lose all jurisdiction over the NGRI, who leaves the courtroom to become a civil patient, and the mental health authorities view their facilities as hospitals full of patients rather than jails full of prisoners, and say that unless an inmate presents an acute medical problem he is not properly their concern. Psychiatry was so widely attacked in the past for overpredicting dangerousness and need for prolonged hospitalization that psychiatrists are now the first to claim that they neither can nor care to predict future behavior. The prevention of criminal activity is a matter for the police and the courts, not for medicine, and even if hospitals wish to retain potentially dangerous NGRIs, the courts themselves have insisted that patients be given periodic reviews at which the burden is on the state to demonstrate a clear and convincing need for continuing involuntary care, based on evidence of dangerous behavior within the recent past—usually within ninety days. An NGRI in remission, then, can go free, unsupervised by anyone, while the courts and the hospitals offer responsibility to each other, but neither is entitled to accept it.

One example of the results brought about by such policies is the case of a Pennsylvania man, pseudonymously called here John Doe. Doe, a happily married man with no previous history of mental illness, was thirty-three years old when, in the autumn of 1978, his behavior grew notably strange and confused. He began to hear voices and believed that people were following him and playing tricks on him. He imagined enemies hiding in empty buildings, and he snipped the wires on his radio and television because, he said, they were talking about him. His delusions of persecution made him violently defensive. He once menaced a neighbor with a butcher knife. At one point when Doe's alarmed family asked a policeman how they could get help for him, the officer replied that under the new commitment laws it was very difficult to hospitalize people, and that Doe would have to commit a crime before the police could intervene.

Doe's mental state continued to deteriorate, and in December his wife persuaded him to go to an outpatient psychiatric clinic. On the day that he was supposed to go, however, Mrs. Doe returned to the house from an errand to find John standing in the street. He jumped into the car and said that while reading the Bible he had found instructions from God to kill eighty-five people; he handed his wife a sheet of paper and pencil: "As I kill the people you just mark them down." The terrified Mrs. Doe tricked John into getting out of the car and raced off to get help, but while she was gone he armed himself with a kitchen knife and set about fulfilling his mission. Seeing a man in the cab of a parked truck, Doe ran over, dragged him out, and stabbed him six times, fatally wounding him. Doe then rushed to a nearby bar, selected a stranger standing at the counter and began to punch and stab him. When the police arrived a few minutes later, Doe had chased his injured victim outside and was kicking him.

Doe was tried in September 1979. Two psychiatrists, one hired by the defense, one an independent court-appointed expert, testified that Doe was a paranoid schizophrenic who had been unable to distinguish between the real and the unreal or between right and wrong at the time of the crime. Based on the persuasive and uncontested evidence, the judge decided that Doe satisfied Pennsylvania's McNaughton Rule and acquitted him by reason of insanity.

Doe was committed to a state mental hospital, where he responded well to medication and treatment. As his condition improved, he was granted grounds privileges and eventually furloughs. Technically, the trial judge should have been notified of any change in Doe's status, but somehow she was not, and the next time the judge heard of him was when she read in the newspaper that in August 1980, less than a year after his acquittal, Doe had returned to the scene of his earlier crime and tried to kill a policeman.

It appeared that Doe had genuinely improved for a time, but then he stopped taking his medication and the paranoid delusions returned. This relapse made him dangerous and, simultaneously, rendered him legally insane, so that when Doe went to trial a second time, in March 1981, a second judge, faced with persuasive and uncontested psychiatric testimony on Doe's quite severe mental illness, felt bound to enter a verdict of not guilty by reason of insanity. Doe returned to the hospital, where he received therapy and medication. Again, he responded well, and at the end of a year staff psychiatrists determined that he had not been a danger to himself or to others within the past three months and was no longer in need of inpatient care. In June 1982, after a hearing in which he was found not to be committable, John Doe was released once more.

There is quite obviously something wrong here, but if, as the evidence seemed to show, Doe truly believed that God had commanded him to kill or that he was defending himself against demonic assailants, one could not in good conscience convict him alongside a defendant who had murdered a truck driver for cash or who tried to kill a policeman while fleeing a burglary scene. We put the criminal in prison for a stipulated term and release him when the sentence expires, not only not caring whether his time in prison has improved him, but resignedly acknowledging the strong likelihood that it has made him worse. This is not an ideal system, but it is consistent with our primary purpose, which is simply to detain and to punish him. The NGRI, on the other hand, is someone whom we have chosen not to punish, but to treat and to release when he is well. But he is also a social problem, and we must balance his needs against those of society.

The answer to this problem is not to hospitalize all NGRIs semipermanently again, nor to eliminate the question itself by abolishing the defense of insanity, convicting mentally ill offenders and, out of sight and out of mind, pretending to treat them in prison. One solution is to provide some individualized mandatory follow-up and supervision for those people who are exculpable at the time of the crime, who with help can function as constructive members of society, but who carry within them a destructive flaw. The law insists that we infringe on the NGRIs' freedom as little as possible, but the fact is that they are not ordinary citizens who should be entitled to absolutely identical rights. The acquittal of an NGRI is specifically predicated on a belief that his crime was not something he fully and rationally chose to do, but that it was the consequence of abnormal psychological factors over which he had no control. If society then offers this person with demonstrable criminal propensities the possibility of quickly regaining his freedom, this release should be predicated on evidence that his criminogenic mental illness is no longer a threat, and an assurance that some responsible agency will be authorized to exercise the minimum supervision necessary to guard against future crimes, and to ensure that the released NGRI now has the sort of control over his acts that other responsible citizens possess.

A decade ago, it was argued that in keeping with such decisions as *Baxstrom* v. *Herold* and *Jackson* v. *Indiana,* the law required identical commitment and release standards for civil and criminal patients. Many states accepted this literally, defense attorneys have argued on these grounds, and hundreds of NGRIs committed under different standards were released as the new attitudes settled into place.

Recently the courts have begun to reinterpret *Baxstrom* and *Jackson* and to state that equal protection considerations do not demand that all people be treated identically, but simply that any differences in treatment must have some reasonable justification. In the course of an insanity trial, the prosecutor still has the burden of proving all material facts of the crime beyond a reasonable doubt, and if he fails in this duty, however disturbed the defendant may be, the jury is obligated to acquit the defendant outright rather than to find him NGRI of a crime they have not been persuaded he did. Thus an NGRI is distinct from a civil involuntary patient not only in that he has been accused of a crime, as was Theon Jackson, but in that, unlike Jackson, it has been proven or stipulated that he did, in fact, commit a criminal act even though there was no conviction. A Second Circuit Court decision[1] used this line of reasoning to justify setting the standard of proof for commitment of NGRIs lower than that for other patients, and the D.C. Circuit Court of Appeals has similarly authorized a higher standard for release.[2] A 1983 Supreme Court decision also found that there were sufficient differences between civil and criminal commitments to justify the use of different criteria.[3]

Several states and, recently, the federal government[4] have extended this principle to permit the imposition of conditions on the release of an NGRI which might well be impermissible if applied to a civil patient. In order to avoid the "revolving door" problem where the patient goes through a regular cycle of recovering in the hospital, relapsing in the community, and eventually being recommitted to start the cycle over again, the courts have authorized a gradual, supervised release. According to the needs of the individual NGRI, the hospital authorities may recommend continuing medication, regular therapy sessions, periodic reports to a social worker, temporary residence in a halfway house, or other conditions. The original sentencing court, perhaps with additional recommendations from the prosecution and defense counsel, can then make these terms part of a binding conditional release order. An NGRI who violates the conditions of his release is thus in contempt of court, and the police have the authority to pick him up and return him to the hospital, where he can be readmitted more easily than under normal civil commitment standards.[5]

Perhaps the best program of this type, that in Maryland, is administered under the auspices of the Clifton T. Perkins Center, the state's maximum security psychiatric facility. At Perkins the NGRI can, as his condition improves, be moved through a succession of progressively less restrictive wards, and eventually given grounds privileges, weekend passes, and placed on a work-release program. When the hospital staff believes he is ready, the NGRI can be put on a renewable five-year conditional release by the sentencing court, with terms recommended by the hospital. A halfway house has been set up in Baltimore for those who have nowhere else to go or who require an intermediate level of daily supervision, and Perkins has established good relations with other social service agencies, enabling the hospital to assist the conditionally released NGRI in such transitional crises as finding work. The location of the Perkins Center near Maryland's major population centers makes follow-up by hospital staff members possible in many cases, and often the same psychiatrist and social worker will follow an NGRI from the time of his postarrest examination through the trial, commitment, and entire conditional release program, giving a reassuring sense of continuity to the patient during this difficult period. Administration of the program by one specialized forensic hospital gives uniformity and the weight of experience to the court recommendations, qualities sometimes lacking in those states with less organized programs, where the arrangements are left to the discretion and knowledge of the sentencing judge, and the nature of conditional release may vary widely according to the local mental health advice available to each individual court.

The state of Oregon has taken a slightly different approach and established an independent state agency, the Psychiatric Security Review Board, which has authority over all NGRI defendants° for a period equal to the maximum sentence the court could have imposed for a conviction on the same charge. The board is composed of a psychiatrist and psychologist familiar with the criminal justice system, a member with experience in probation and parole, a lawyer who practices criminal law, and a representative of the general public[7]—a diverse group intended to furnish the best knowledge and experience of both the mental health and criminal justice systems. The primary concern of the board, according to the law that established it, is the protection of society rather than purely medical considerations of the NGRI's state, and it has

---

° The verdict in Oregon has actually been changed to "not responsible by reason of insanity." Several organizations, including the National Mental Health Association,[6] have recommended the general adoption of this verdict since, though the terms "not responsible" and "not guilty" are legally identical, popular usage of the word "guilty" is often synonymous with "committed the act," and a "not guilty" verdict appears to deny that anything ever happened.

wide discretionary powers to establish conditional release terms oriented toward this goal.

Psychiatry is not good at predicting the future behavior of patients who are launched into unknown conditions, but a psychiatrist or social worker can make useful determinations about the mental state of a patient under regular supervision. The relative newness of the conditional release programs and the great variation between them renders it impossible to make accurate remarks about their overall success rates, but initial results seem encouraging.[8] Recidivism among conditionally released NGRIs is lower than among paroled convicts or unconditionally released NGRIs. They show a good rate of compliance with the medical terms of their release, and in those cases where rehospitalization has been necessary, it was achieved with relative ease and rapidity.

Though NGRIs on conditional release have the right to petition the court for reduction or removal of the conditions, there have been few challenges thus far, perhaps because conditions are kept to an essential minimum, have a therapeutic rather than a punitive character, and because it is clear even to the patient himself that compliance will help him to avoid the more onerous possibility of rehospitalization. One can only hope that, in the years to come, legislatures will move to develop such programs for dealing with NGRIs rather than succumbing to rare but well-publicized disasters and worrying over troublesome and, it would seem, ultimately useless alterations in tests and verdicts.

We ought to retain the insanity defense because it permits us to forgive where there is no blame, and gives us an opportunity, however crude and circumscribed, to examine our moral and scientific understanding of the relationship between men and their laws. It is a social manifestation of sentiments each of us finds within himself as he evaluates his own actions and those of people around him. A draconian policy that never looked within the mind of the doer to determine the purpose and inner responsibility behind an act would achieve public security at the expense of compassion and individual rights and would violate the ageless credo that there is no justice that is not tempered with mercy. But to flock to the opposite extreme is sheer madness, for mercy run wild and untempered by justice is neither just nor merciful. Once we have made the very crude decision not to impose blame, we cannot naively absolve the defendant of all responsibility as well. He is free, it is true, of criminal responsibility and legal guilt, but there is a moral and practical duty imposed on the defendant, on those around him, and on the law, to take reasonable precautions to ensure that society's compassion is not rewarded by further harm. We have failed lamentably in dealing with convicts, whom we punish at great expense and to no avail, but the one small area of the insanity defense presents an opportunity to understand what caused a given offense and to learn to prevent it from happening again.

SOURCE NOTES

INTRODUCTION

1. *New York Times*, June 23, 1982, p. B6.
2. Radio Address of the President to the Nation, September 11, 1982.
3. *New York Times*, September 12, 1982, p. 37.
4. *Newsweek*, September 20, 1982, p. 30.
5. Pasewark, Richard A., & Pantle, Mark L., "Insanity Plea: Legislators' View," 136 *American Journal of Psychiatry* 222 (1979).
6. Pasewark, Richard A., & Seidenzahl, D., "Opinions Concerning the Insanity Plea and Criminality Among Mental Patients," 7 *Bulletin of the American Academy of Psychiatry and the Law* 199 (1979).
7. See, e.g., Pasewark, Richard A., "Insanity Plea: a review of the research literature," 9 *Journal of Psychiatry and Law* 357 (1981); and Steadman, Henry J. et al., "Mentally Disordered Offenders," 6 *Law and Human Behavior* 31 (1982).
8. Letter from Assistant Attorney General Robert McConnell to Sen. Strom Thurmond, in *The Insanity Defense*, Hearings before the Committee on the Judiciary, U.S. Senate, pp. 51–52.
9. Steadman et al., op. cit.

1. THE ORIGINS OF THE INSANITY DEFENSE

1. Holmes, Oliver, *The Common Law*, Boston, Little, Brown & Co., 1881, p. 3.
2. Plato, *The Laws*, IX, 864, trans. Trevor J. Saunders, Penguin Books, 1970, pp. 376–77.
3. Cited in Biggs, John, *The Guilty Mind*, New York, Harcourt, Brace & Co., 1955, p. 82.
4. Cited in Walker, Nigel, *Crime and Insanity in England*, Edinburgh, Edinburgh University Press, 1968, vol. I, p. 19.
5. Ibid., pp. 20–23.

6. Calendar of Close Rolls, Edward I; 7 Edw. I 518 (1278).

7. Letter of Charles Doe to Isaac Ray, May 18, 1868, cited in Reik, Louis E., "The Doe-Ray Correspondence: A Pioneer Collaboration in the Jurisprudence of Mental Disease," 63 *Yale Law Journal* 189 (1953).

8. Cited in Hawkins, 1 *Pleas of the Crown* 2 (1716).

9. Quoted in Walker, op. cit., vol. I, p. 41.

10. Blackstone, 4 *Commentaries on the Laws of England* 23–24 (1765).

2. THE EARLY ENGLISH INSANITY TRIALS

1. *Rex* v. *Arnold*, 16 How. St. Tr. 695 (1724).

2. *Trial of Earl Ferrers*, 19 How. St. Tr. 886 (1760).

3. *Trial of James Hadfield*, 27 How. St. Tr. 1282 (1800).

4. *Trial of Sir A. Gordon Kinloch*, 25 How. St. Tr. 891 (1795).

5. 39 & 40 George III, c. 94.

6. Campbell, John, *The Lives of the Lord Chancellors and Keepers of the Great Seal of England*, London, John Murray, 1847, vol. VI, p. 527.

7. *Times*, (London), May 13, 1812.

8. Ibid.

9. Ibid.

10. Ibid.

11. *Reg.* v. *Edward Oxford*, 9 C. & P. 525 (1840)

12. Case notes dated February 16, 1854, courtesy of Patricia Allderidge, Archivist of Bethlem Royal Hospital.

13. Information courtesy of Thomas Maguire, Consultant Forensic Psychiatrist, Broadmoor Hospital.

3. THE TRIAL OF DANIEL MCNAUGHTON

1. Correspondence reproduced in Frankfurter, Felix, *Of Law and Life and Other Things That Matter*, Cambridge, Mass., Harvard University Press, 1965.

2. Diamond, Bernard, "On the Spelling of Daniel M'Naghten's Name," in West, Donald, & Walk, Alexander, *Daniel McNaughton: His Trial and the Aftermath*, London, Gaskell Books, 1977, pp. 86–90.

3. *Daniel M'Naghten's Case*, 10 Clark & Finnelly 200; 8 Eng. Rep. R. 718 (1843).

4. Quoted in Ormrod, Sir Roger, "The McNaughton Case and Its Predecessors," in West & Walk, op. cit., pp. 8–9.

5. Benson, A. C. (ed.), *The Letters of Queen Victoria*, New York, Longman's, Green, & Co., 1907, vol. I, p. 587.

6. *Hansard's Parliamentary Debates*, Third Series, vol. 67, p. 722.

7. Ibid., p. 732.

8. Rollin, Henry R. "McNaughton's Madness," in West & Walk, op. cit., p. 91.

4. PSYCHIATRY AND THE LAW

1. *George Frederick Cooke's Case*, 1 City Hall Recorder (New York) 5 (1816).

2. Cited in Bucknill, John C., *Unsoundness of Mind in Relation to Criminal Acts*, Philadelphia, T. & J.W. Johnson & Co., 1856, p. 16.

3. Ray, Isaac, *A Treatise on the Medical Jurisprudence of Insanity* (ed. Winfred Overholser), Cambridge, Mass., Belknap Press, 1962, p. 93.

4. Ibid., pp. 139–40.

5. Ibid., pp. 44–45.

6. Ibid., p. 49.

7. *Boardman* v. *Woodman*, 47 N.H. 120 (1866).

8. Ibid. at 150.

9. Reik, Louis E., "The Doe-Ray Correspondence: A Pioneer Collaboration in the Jurisprudence of Mental Disease," 63 *Yale Law Journal* 183, 185 (1953).

10. Letter of January 18, 1869, ibid., at 193.

11. *State* v. *Pike*, 49 N.H. 399 (1869).

12. Ibid., at 402.

13. Ibid., at 441.

14. *State* v. *Jones*, 50 N.H. 369 (1871).

15. Weihofen, Henry, "The Flowering of New Hampshire," 22 *University of Chicago Law Review* 356 (1955).

16. Letter of January 12, 1869, in Reik, op. cit., at 193.

17. Maudsley, Henry, *Responsibility in Mental Disease*, London, H.S. King, 1874, p. 143.

18. Winslow, Forbes, *The Plea of Insanity in Criminal Cases*, London, H. Renshaw, 1843, p. 74.

19. Ray, op. cit., p. 192.
20. *Regina* v. *Oxford,* 9 C. & P. 546 (1840).
21. *Commonwealth* v. *Rogers,* 7 Metcalf 502 (Mass. 1844).
22. *State* v. *Harrison,* 36 W. Va. 729 (1892).
23. Cited in *People* v. *Hubert,* 119 Cal. 216 (1897).
24. *Rex* v. *Creighton,* 14 Can. Cr. Cas. 349 (Canada 1908).

5. OPPOSITION TO THE INSANITY DEFENSE

1. *State* v. *Sikora,* 44 N.J. 453 (1965).
2. Twain, Mark, "A New Crime," in *The Writings of Mark Twain,* Author's National Edition, New York, Harper & Bros., 1909, vol. XIX, p. 244.
3. Cited in Rosenberg, Charles E., *The Trial of the Assassin Guiteau,* Chicago, University of Chicago Press, 1968, p. 98.
4. *Hansard's Parliamentary Debates,* Third Series, vol. 67, p. 424.
5. *Times* (London), April 19, 1882.
6. *The Letters of Queen Victoria,* Second Series, London, John Murray, 1928, vol. III, p. 269.
7. Ibid., p. 278.
8. 46 & 47 Vict. c. 38.
9. Cited in Glueck, Sheldon, *Law and Psychiatry,* Baltimore, Johns Hopkins Press, 1962.
10. *Felstead* v. *Rex,* A.C. 534 (1914).
11. Ibid., at 542.
12. 81 *Central Law Journal* 23 (1915).
13. Cited in 81 *Central Law Journal* 23 (1915).
14. Quoted in Mooney, Michael M., *Evelyn Nesbit and Stanford White,* New York, Wm. Morrow & Co., Inc. 1976, p. 262.
15. "Report of the Special Committee on the Commitment and Discharge of the Criminal Insane," December 30, 1909, in *Report of the New York State Bar Association,* vol. 33, (1910) p. 396.
16. Ibid., at 400.
17. *Laws of 1909,* sec. 7 (Rem. & Bal. Code sec. 2259).
18. *Laws of 1909,* sec. 31 (Rem. & Bal. Code sec. 2283).
19. *Report of the New York State Bar Association,* op. cit., p. 402.
20. Cited in Sayre, Francis B., "Public Welfare Offenses," 33 *Columbia Law Review* 55 (1933).

21. *State* v. *Strasburg*, 60 Wash. 106, 123 (1910).

22. *Laws of 1928*, Chapter 75.

23. *Sinclair* v. *State*, 161 Miss. 142, 143 (1931).

24. Ibid., at 174.

25. Cal. Stat. 1925, chap. 346, p. 623.

26. Louisell, David W., & Hazard, Geoffrey C., "Insanity as a Defense: The Bifurcated Trial," 49 *California Law Review* 807 (1961).

27. California Commission for the Reform of Criminal Procedure, *Report*, pp. 16–17 (1927).

28. Cal. Pen. Code, secs. 1016 & 1026 (1927).

29. *Hopt* v. *People*, 104 U.S. 631, 634 (1881).

30. *Sabens* v. *U.S.*, 40 App. D.C. 440 (1913).

31. See Weihofen, Henry & Overholser, Winfred, "Mental Disorder Affecting the Degree of a Crime," 56 *Yale Law Journal* 967 (1947).

32. *People* v. *Harris*, 169 Cal. 66 (1914).

33. *People* v. *Troche*, 206 Cal. 35 (1928) and *People* v. *Leong Fook*, 206 Cal. 64 (1928).

34. *Troche*, at 42.

35. *Troche*, at 44.

36. *Troche*, at 47.

37. *People* v. *Wells*, 33 Cal.2d 330 (1949).

38. See also *People* v. *Danielly*, 33 Cal.2d 362 (1949), decided on the same day as *Wells*.

39. *Wells*, at 350–51.

40. *Wells*, at 360.

41. Diamond, Bernard, "Criminal Responsibility of the Mentally Ill," 14 *Stanford Law Review* 59, 75 (1961).

42. *People* v. *Gorshen*, 31 Cal.2d 716 (1959).

43. *People* v. *Wolff*, 61 Cal.2d 795 (1964).

44. Ibid., at 821. Italics in original.

45. *People* v. *Conley*, 64 Cal.2d 310, 322 (1966).

46. Johnson, Phillip E., "The Accidental Decision and How It Happens," 65 *California Law Review* 231, 242 (1977).

6. THE *DURHAM* EXPERIMENT

1. Royal Commission on Capital Punishment, 1949–1953, *Report*, London, Her Majesty's Stationery Office, 1953.

2. Guttmacher, Manfred, "Why Psychiatrists Do Not Like to Testify in Court," 1 *Practical Lawyer* 50, 51–52 (May 1955).

3. Cited in Wiseman, F., "Psychiatry and Law: Use and Abuse of Psychiatry in a Murder Case," 118 *American Journal of Psychiatry* 289, 292 (1961).

4. Zilboorg, Gregory, "Misconceptions of Legal Insanity," 9 *American Journal of Orthopsychiatry* 540, 552 (1939).

5. Royal Commission on Capital Punishment, *Report*, op. cit., p. 82.

6. Ibid., p. 82.

7. Ibid., p. 102.

8. Diamond, Bernard, "Criminal Responsibility of the Mentally Ill," 14 *Stanford Law Review* 59, 84 (1961).

9. Interview, October 14, 1981.

10. Ibid.

11. *Durham* v. *U.S.*, 214 F.2d 862, 864 (1954).

12. *Tatum* v. *U.S.*, 88 U.S. App. D.C. 386 (1951).

13. *Durham*, at 868.

14. *Durham*, at 874–75.

15. *Durham*, at 875.

16. *Durham*, at 875.

17. Bazelon, David L., "Equal Justice for the Unequal," Isaac Ray Lectureship Award Series, 1961, unpublished manuscript, p. 11.

18. *Stewart* v. *U.S.*, 214 F.2d 879 (1954).

19. *Carter* v. *U.S.*, 252 F.2d 608, 617 (1957).

20. *Douglas* v. *U.S.*, 239 F.2d 52 (1956).

21. *Campbell* v. *U.S.*, 307 F.2d 597, 609 (1962).

22. *U.S.* v. *Blocker*, 274 F.2d 572 (1959).

23. Burger, Warren, "Psychiatrists, Lawyers, and the Courts," 28 Federal Probation 3, 5 (1964).

24. Amicus Curiae by William H. Dempsey, Jr., Appendix A, filed in *U.S.* v. *Brawner*, 471 F.2d 969 (1972).

25. *Washington* v. *U.S.*, 390 F.2d 444, 449 (1967).

26. Ibid., at 448.

27. Ibid.

28. *McDonald* v. *U.S.*, 312 F.2d 847 (1962).

29. Ibid., at 851.

30. Ibid.

31. *Washington*, op. cit., at 458.

32. Ibid., at 457.

33. *U.S.* v. *Brawner*, 471 F.2d 969 (1972).

34. See Wechsler, Herbert, "Codification of Criminal Law in the United States: The Model Penal Code," 68 *Columbia Law Review* 1425, 1442 (1968).

35. American Law Institute, *Model Penal Code*, Tentative Draft 4, 1955, sec. 4.01.

7. THE JURY AND THE INSANITY DEFENSE

1. Goldstein, Abraham, *The Insanity Defense*, New Haven, Yale University Press, 1967, pp. 53–54.

2. Matthews, Arthur R., *Mental Disability and the Criminal Law*, Chicago, American Bar Foundation, 1970, p. 44.

3. Interview, March 27, 1982.

4. American Law Institute, *Model Penal Code*, Tentative Draft 4, sec. 4.01, alternative (1) (a).

5. Cited in Taft, Charles P., "So This Is Justice!" *World's Work*, vol. 56, p. 96 (1928).

6. Ibid., p. 98.

7. "How to Stop 'Remus Verdicts,' " *Literary Digest*, vol. 96, p. 14 (June 23, 1928).

8. See Kalven, Harry Jr., & Zeisel, Hans, *The American Jury*, Boston, Little, Brown & Co., 1966, and Simon, Rita J., *The Jury: Its Role in American Society*, Lexington, Mass., Lexington Books, 1980.

9. Arens, Richard, et al., "Jurors, Jury Charges, and Insanity," 14 *Catholic University Law Review* 1 (1965).

10. Ibid., at 26.

11. Simon, Rita J., *The Jury and the Defense of Insanity*, Boston, Little, Brown & Co., 1967.

12. Ibid., p. 147.

8. INCOMPETENCY TO STAND TRIAL

1. Unpublished figures, from Written Statement of Joseph H. Rodriguez, Public Advocate (State of New Jersey), submitted to the Senate Judiciary Committee, August 5, 1982, p. 16a.

2. Matthews, Arthur R., *Mental Disability and the Criminal Law*, Chicago, American Bar Foundation, 1970, p. 48.

3. Morris, Grant H., "Confusion of Confinement Syndrome *Extended:* The Treatment of Mentally Ill 'Non-Criminal Criminals' in New York," 18 *Buffalo Law Review* 393, 425–26, (1960).

4. Thornberry, Terence P., & Jacoby, Joseph E., *The Criminally Insane: A Community Follow-up of Mentally Ill Offenders,* Chicago, University of Chicago Press, 1979, p. 6.

5. Interview, March 26, 1982.

6. 4 Blackstone 24 (1765).

7. Consolidated Statutes, vol. 2, sec. 6236 (1919).

8. General Laws (1923) sec. 4909.

9. *Johnson* v. *State,* 57 Fla. 18 (1909).

10. Smith, Charles E., "Psychiatry in Corrections," 120 *American Journal of Psychiatry* 1046 (1964).

11. Scheidemandel, Patricia, & Kanno, Charles, *The Mentally Ill Offender: A Survey of Treatment Programs,* Washington, D.C., Joint Information Service, APA–NIMH, 1966.

12. Note: "Incompetency to Stand Trial," 81 *Harvard Law Review* 454 n.2 (1967–68).

13. Rosenberg, Arthur H., "Competency for Trial—Who Knows Best?" 6 *Criminal Law Bulletin,* 577 (1970).

14. Hess, John H., & Thomas, Herbert E., "Incompetency to Stand Trial: Procedures, Results, and Problems," 119 *American Journal of Psychiatry* 713 (1963).

15. McGarry, A. Louis, "Competency for Trial and Due Process Via the State Hospital," 122 *American Journal of Psychiatry* 623 (1965).

16. McGarry, A. Louis, "Demonstration and Research in Competency for Trial and Mental Illness: Review and Preview," 49 *Boston University Law Review* 46 (1969).

17. Hess & Thomas, op. cit.

18. Ibid., at 717.

19. McGarry (1965), at 624.

20. Gobert, J., "Competency to Stand Trial—a Pre- and Post-*Jackson* Analysis," 40 *Tennessee Law Review* 659 (1973).

21. Hess & Thomas, op. cit., at 715.

22. Cited in Association of the Bar of the City of New York, *Mental Illness, Due Process and the Criminal Defendant,* New York, Fordham University Press, 1968, p. 72.

23. *New York Times,* May 1, 1964, p. 71.

24. Association of the Bar of the City of New York, op. cit., p. 73.

25. Hess & Thomas, op. cit.

26. McGarry (1969), at 50, n. 20.

27. Hess & Thomas, op. cit., 714–15.

28. Eizenstat, Stuart E., "Mental Competency to Stand Trial," 4 *Harvard Civil Rights-Civil Liberties Law Review* 379 (1969).

29. See, e.g., Halpern, A. L., "Use and Misuse of Psychiatry in Competency Examinations of Criminal Defendants," 5 *Psychiatric Annals* 8 (1975); Slovenko, Ralph, "Developing Law on Competency to Stand Trial," 5 *Journal of Psychiatry and Law* 165 (1977); and Szasz, Thomas, *Psychiatric Justice*, New York, Macmillan, 1965.

30. Harvard Medical School, Laboratory of Community Psychiatry, "Competency to Stand Trial and Mental Illness," Washington, D.C., NIMH, U.S. Gov. Printing Office, 1973, pp. 55–56.

31. Ennis, Bruce, *Prisoners of Psychiatry*, New York, Harcourt Brace Jovanovich, Inc., 1972.

32. *U.S. ex rel. von Wolfersdorf* v. *Johnston*, 317 F.Supp. 67 (1970).

33. *New York Times*, December 6, 1972, p. 51.

9. THE REVOLVING DOOR

1. *Baxstrom* v. *Herold*, 383 U.S. 107 (1966).

2. *Baxstrom* v. *Herold*, at 111–12.

3. Steadman, Henry J., and Keveles, C., "The Community Adjustment and Criminal Activity of the Baxstrom Patients: 1966–1970," 129 *American Journal of Psychiatry* 80 (1972).

4. *Bolton* v. *Harris*, 395 F.2d 642 (D.C. Cir. 1968).

5. *Dusky* v. *U.S.*, 362 U.S. 402 (1960).

6. Robey, Ames, "Criteria for Competency to Stand Trial: A Checklist for Psychiatrists," 122 *American Journal of Psychiatry* 616 (1965).

7. *Comm.* v. *Druken*, 254 N.E.2d 779 (Mass. 1970).

8. Harvard Medical School, Laboratory of Community Psychiatry, *Competency to Stand Trial and Mental Illness*, Washington, D.C., Government Printing Office, NIMH, Crime and Delinquency Series, 1973, p. 50.

9. N.Y. Crim. Proc. Law, sec. 730.50 (1971).

10. *Jackson* v. *Indiana*, 406 U.S. 715 (1972).

11. *Jackson*, at 718–19.

12. *Jackson*, at 724.

13. *Jackson*, at 738.

14. *Jackson*, at 740.

10. GUILTY BUT MENTALLY ILL

1. Mitchell, William J., "Freedom Didn't Help Ex-Patient," *Detroit Free Press*, June 15, 1975, p. 13-A.
2. Ibid.
3. *People* v. *McQuillan*, 392 Mich. 511 (1974).
4. *McQuillan*, at 515.
5. Interview, March 26, 1982.
6. Forensic Center Budget Report for 1974–75, p. 159.
7. Ibid., p. 157.
8. Robey, Ames, & Pogany, E., "The NGRI commitment and *McQuillan*," unpublished DMH study (1974), cited in Robey, Ames, "Guilty But Mentally Ill," 6 *Bulletin of the American Academy of Psychiatry and the Law* 376 (1978).
9. *Detroit Free Press*, March 22, 1975.
10. *Detroit Free Press*, February 5, 1976.
11. Mitchell, William J., "The McQuillan Ruling and John McGee: Why One Man's Violence Went Unchecked," *Detroit Free Press*, June 15, 1975, p. 1-D.
12. *Detroit Free Press*, March 7, 1975.
13. *Detroit Free Press*, March 15, 1975.
14. *Detroit Free Press*, June 15, 1975.
15. *Detroit Free Press*, March 15, 1975.
16. *Detroit Free Press*, October 8, 1976.
17. 70 MCLA 768.36 (1).
18. Robey (1978), at 377.
19. *Chicago Tribune*, May 13, 1977.
20. *Chicago Tribune*, April 18, 1978.
21. Ibid.
22. Nesson, Charles, "A Needed Verdict: Guilty but Insane," *New York Times*, July 1, 1982.
23. Smith, Gare A., & James A. Hall, "Evaluating Michigan's Guilty But Mentally Ill Verdict: An Empirical Study," 16 *University of Michigan Journal of Law Reform* 77 (1982).
24. Ibid., at 100.
25. Interview, March 27, 1982.
26. Interview, March 29, 1982.

11. ABOLISHING THE DEFENSE

1. Testimony of Alan Stone, M.D., *Limiting the Insanity Defense,* Hearings before the Subcommittee on Criminal Law of the Committee on the Judiciary, United States Senate, Washington, D.C., U.S. Government Printing Office, 1983 (hereinafter referred to as *Hearings—I*), p. 255.

2. S. 2678, by Senators Nunn, Chiles, and Randolph, June 24, 1982.

3. Letter from Rep. Michael Keedy, January 13, 1982.

4. Ibid.

5. Ibid.

6. Statement of Hon. William French Smith, *The Insanity Defense,* Hearings before the Committee on the Judiciary, United States Senate, Washington, D.C., U.S. Government Printing Office, 1982 (hereinafter referred to as *Hearings—II*), p. 30.

7. Statement of Hon. Rudolph W. Giuliani, Associate Attorney General, *Hearings—II*, p. 41.

8. Ibid., p. 41.

9. Statement of Randolph A. Read, M.D., *Hearings—II*, p. 57.

10. Testimony of Jonas Rappeport, M.D., *Hearings—I*, p. 249.

11. Keedy, Edwin, "Insanity and Criminal Responsibility," 7 *Journal of Criminal Law and Criminology* 484 (1916).

12. Keedy, Edwin, "Insanity and Criminal Responsibility," 30 *Harvard Law Review* 536, 558-60 (1917).

13. Keedy (1916), op. cit., p. 488.

14. Goldstein, Joseph, & Katz, Jay, "Abolish 'The Insanity Defense'—Why Not?" 72 *Yale Law Journal* 853 (1963).

15. *Washington Post,* March 15, 1973, "Nixon Details Anti-Crime Law Package."

16. Bazelon, David, "The Morality of the Criminal Law," 49 *Southern California Law Review* 385, 397 (1976).

17. *Hearings—II*, p. 37.

18. Testimony of Abraham Goldstein, Attorney General's Task Force on Violent Crime, Hearings, Atlanta, Ga., May 20, 1981, unpublished transcript, p. 113.

19. Kadish, Sanford, "The Decline of Innocence," 26 *Cambridge Law Journal* 273, 280 (1968).

20. *Leland* v. *Oregon,* 343 U.S. 790 (1952).

21. See, e.g., *In re Winship,* 397 U.S. 358 (1957) and *Sandstrom* v. *Montana,* 442 U.S. 510 (1979).

22. Lewin, Travis, "Psychiatric Evidence in Criminal Cases for Purposes other than the Defense of Insanity," 26 *Syracuse Law Review* 1051, 1087 (1975).

23. Kadish, op. cit., p. 282.

24. Interview, July 7, 1982.

25. Interviews, June 3, 1983.

26. Personal communications from Michael Keedy and Marc Racicot. See, for example, *State* v. *Mercer*, 625 P.2d 44, 49 (1981).

27. Newspaper clipping, source unknown, courtesy of Michael Keedy.

28. Sample instructions can be found in the Statement of John Maynard, *Hearings—II*, pp. 241–48.

29. By the end of 1984 Montana's legislation had survived five challenges: *State* v. *Mercer*, 625 P.2d 44 (Mont. 1981), *State* v. *Doney*, 636 P.2d 1377 (Mont. 1981), *State* v. *Zampich*, 667 P.2d 955 (Mont. 1983), *State* v. *Watson*, 686 P.2d 879 (Mont. 1984), and *State* v. *Korell* __ P.2d __ (Mont. 1984). None of them dealt with the precise quality of psychiatric evidence that should be admissible under a *mens rea* test.

30. Testimony of Richard J. Bonnie, *Hearings—II*, pp. 258–59.

31. Statement of Richard J. Bonnie, *Hearings—II*, p. 273.

32. Ibid., p. 274.

33. 46-14-312 MCA (1979).

12. THE QUESTION OF DISPOSITION

1. *Warren* v. *Harvey*, 632 F.2d 925 (2nd Cir. 1980).

2. *U.S.* v. *Ecker*, 543 F.2d 178 (D.C. Cir. 1976).

3. *Jones* v. *U.S.* 51 U.S.L.W. 5041 (1983).

4. Insanity Defense Reform Act of 1984, enacted October 12, 1984.

5. See Weiner, Barbara A., "Not Guilty by Reason of Insanity: A Sane Approach," 56 *Chicago–Kent Law Review* 1057 (1980).

6. National Commission on the Insanity Defense, *Myths & Realities*, Arlington, Va., National Mental Health Association, 1983.

7. Or. Rev. Stat. 161.385.

8. See, e.g., Testimony of James L. Cavanaugh, Jr., M.D., Hearings before the Subcommittee on Criminal Law of the Committee on the Judiciary, United States Senate, Washington, D.C., Government Printing Office, 1983, p. 225; Statement of Stuart B. Silver, M.D., ibid., p. 378; Rogers, Jeffrey L., & Bloom, Jeffrey D., "Characteristics

of Persons Committed to Oregon's Psychiatric Security Review Board," 10 *Bulletin of the American Academy of Psychiatry and Law* 155 (1982); and Bloom, Jeffrey D., Rogers, Jeffrey L., and Manson, Spero M., "After Oregon's Insanity Defense: A Comparison of Conditional Release and Hospitalization," 5 *International Journal of Law and Psychiatry* 391 (1982).

INDEX

Index

Index